WHAT WE BELIEVE
THE PATH OF BUDDHISM

WHAT WE BELIEVE
THE PATH OF BUDDHISM

George Chryssides

THE SAINT ANDREW PRESS
· EDINBURGH ·

First published in 1988 by
THE SAINT ANDREW PRESS
121 George Street, Edinburgh

Copyright © 1988 George Chryssides

ISBN 0 7152 0619 2

294.3

British Library Cataloguing in Publication Data
Chryssides, George
What We Believe (series): The Path of Buddhism.
1. Buddhism
I. Title
294.3   BQ4012

ISBN 0–7152–0619–2

Filmset by J&L Composition Ltd
Filey, North Yorkshire
Printed by Thomson Litho, East Kilbride

Contents

List of Illustrations

Preface

In its *Guidelines on Dialogue with People of Other Faiths*, the World Council of Churches recommends that adherents to other faiths should be free to 'define themselves'. This means that if we want to understand the beliefs and practices of a Buddhist, we should ask a Buddhist rather than a Hindu, a Muslim or a Christian.

As a non-Buddhist writing about Buddhism, my aim has been two-fold. *First*, I have tried to convey some of the fundamental beliefs and practices of various forms of Buddhism to the general reader who does not necessarily have any previous knowledge. *Second*, in the spirit of the WCC Guidelines, I have attempted to write something which Buddhists will recognise as an accurate portrait of themselves.

Many Buddhists have helped to ensure that my descriptions of Buddhism are as accurate as possible, and I am grateful for the help — and often hospitality — which they have provided. The Ven M Vajiragnana, Head of the London Buddhist Vihara, took a keen interest in the book's progress, discussed numerous questions with me, and granted me unlimited access to the Vihara's library. Kittisaro Bhikkhu, Senior Incumbent of the Devon Vihara, patiently answered many points about the Theravada Tradition. Philip Eden (Vice-President of the Buddhist Society of Great Britain), Russell Webb (Editor, *Buddhist Studies Review*) and his wife Sara, read and commented on earlier versions of the manuscript. Dr Paul Williams of Bristol University, himself a Buddhist in the Tibetan tradition, went through an earlier version with a fine toothcomb, and made many suggestions.

I am also grateful to Bill Picard and Mike Hughes for giving me observations from the Zen tradition. Dick Causton and John Delnevo of the Nichiren Shoshu of the United Kingdom (NSUK) commented at length on Chapter Nine, and presented me with a generous quantity of their own literature. Dave Pengelly, Secretary of the Plymouth Buddhist Group, made helpful comments from the view-point of the Theravadin layman. These are only some of the many Buddhists to whom I am indebted, and I only hope I have repaid them in part by producing a book which will help others to understand the path of Buddhism.

Among non-Buddhist friends I am particularly grateful to Mrs Mairi Levitt and Dr Linda Moss for their interest, encouragement and valuable comments throughout the course of writing.

To cite so many names is not to suggest that this book carries their 'seal of approval'. No one but myself can bear the final responsibility for what is written here. Like Christians, Buddhists have differing beliefs and practices, and it was inevitable that on occasions I was told different things by different people. Sometimes I had to decide who was more probably correct, but wherever possible I have attempted simply to highlight the points at which certain Buddhists disagree, and to give their reasons.

One or two words about my approach are needed. *First,* when writing about Buddhist teachings I have not always issued disclaimers like 'allegedly', 'supposedly' or 'it is held that . . .'. This would not only be tiresome to the reader but insulting to Buddhists. When I talk, for example, of Buddhists recognising the truth of their teachings through meditation, this does not mean that I accept Buddhist teachings to be 'true'; it is merely a shorthand way of reporting what a Buddhist would say, if asked. At no point have I raised questions about truth or falsity: the aim of the book is to make understanding possible; only when that has occurred is anyone in a position to decide his or her personal attitude towards Buddhism.

Second, it would be inappropriate to use the abbreviations 'AD' and 'BC' after dates, since a Buddhist does not acknowledge Jesus Christ as Lord. Instead, I have substituted 'CE' and 'BCE' ('Christian Era' and 'Before Christian Era'), in common with many current writers on world religions.

I have used 'inclusive language' throughout, but with some deliberate exceptions. Where groups of people are typically male (such as Theravadin monks), it would be misleading and perverse to say 'he or she' in these contexts.

Finally, for those who are sensitive to more technical points, I had to decide on the language in which Buddhist key terms should be expressed. Since Buddhism has flourished in cultures which have used many different languages, this was not an easy decision, and readers might have been confused by arrays of alternative names and spellings. I have normally used Sanskrit terms, despite the fact that Theravada Buddhists would talk about *nibbana* rather than *nirvana*, and *kamma* rather than *karma*. However, where a word is more characteristically found in a non-Sanskrit tradition (such as Tibetan and Japanese), I have used that tradition's language. Tibetan names can look particularly terrifying, but there is little I can do about this: I did not invent them, nor can I change them. The best I can do is to offer the simplest spelling which makes for the easiest and most accurate pronunciation.

George Chryssides, 1987

Introduction

It is difficult to know where to begin when introducing any religion. If Christians were asked to present Christianity (in its entirety) to total strangers, should they describe Syrian Orthodoxy or the Salvation Army? Should they mention Augustine, St Thomas Aquinas, Luther and Calvin, whom most Christians have never read at first hand? Or would it be better to comment on the average member in the pew who attends a Woman's Guild or Fellowship Meeting? Perhaps it would be preferable to give the story of the Old and New Testaments: this might seem a promising approach, but, even so, how many Christians have read the Bible from cover to cover?

To describe Buddhism presents the same problems magnified to an infinitely greater degree. There are many more brands of Buddhism than of Christianity, but if we described these, we would not be giving a picture of 'what every Buddhist knows', since many Buddhists are only familiar with their own variety. We could study some of the scholars, yet many Buddhists have never heard of Nagarjuna or Tsongkhapa, great though these men were. We could try examining the scriptures, but different Buddhists use different religious writings, and the total amount of scripture is so vast that no scholar, either eastern or western, has read it all. If we pay too much attention to the monk, we neglect what it is like to be a Buddhist lay person. If we focus too narrowly on the folk practices and pageantry of the various festivals, we might be left with the impression that Buddhism is an unreflecting faith, practised by fairly simple folk.

In the end, any writer must compromise. I have chosen to present a cross-section of Buddhism, looking at its origins and development, its beliefs and practices, and then the various traditions that exist. I have tried to view it from the vantage point of the monk, the lay person, the scholar, the person who is born in a Buddhist country, and the westerner who comes into contact with Buddhist people or ideas. To attempt all this may be over-ambitious, and I am aware that where I have stopped to comment on the ideas of some of Buddhism's great thinkers, there is the risk of losing the attention of readers who prefer more of a travelogue to the more abstract ideas of philosophers. However, to ignore the latter could easily perpetuate the myth that we in the West have a monopoly of solid reflection on religious matters. On the few occasions when the going is slightly tougher, I have alerted those readers who may be less at home with abstractions, so that they may skip through these more intellectual forests to the next clearing.

1

The Life and Times of the Buddha

Those who are more familiar with Christianity than with any other faith often find Buddhism a very strange religion. It does not appear to have a God. It denies that there are eternal souls. The Buddha was merely a man who accomplished nothing that could not be achieved by any other mortal. Men and women, apparently, must save themselves, rather than be saved by the Buddha. Its constant stress on 'suffering' often caused western missionaries to preach that Buddhism only offered despair, whereas Christianity offered hope. If all this is so, it may be asked, how can Buddhism even count as a religion at all?

To some, the notions of 'no self', 'no God', 'no external saviour' appal. To others, they appeal, and as a result these westerners find themselves drawn to Buddhism. Those who come do so for different reasons. Since Buddhism occurs in many varieties, it can satisfy many different spiritual needs which people feel.

It is the life of the traditional Theravadin monk which has captured the imagination of many popular writers. However, Theravada Buddhism is only one Buddhist tradition. The Mahayana forms include the Tibetans, with their complex and highly symbolic rituals, with the Dalai Lama as their spiritual head. Then there is the Zen Buddhist, who tries to overcome the intellect by attempting to solve seemingly senseless puzzles. There are the 'Pure Land' sects, which made the Buddhas objects of devotion, and there are the Nichiren sects of Japan, who seem to have material goals rather than 'other-worldly' ones.

Some seekers are attracted by Buddhism's meditative practices. Some have felt that elements of its teaching — such as rebirth — made sense to them. Others are attracted to the elaborate ritual devised by the Tibetans. Some find their way in through the peace movement, while, by contrast, others have studied oriental techniques of self-defence such as aikido or karate, and felt that they wanted to know more about the religion which is associated with them. For some western Buddhists it was not really a matter of conversion at all, they will say; when they discovered Buddhism, they recognised in its teachings something which they had believed all along: it was as if they had always been Buddhists without knowing it.

A few westerners turn to Buddhism in order to cope with emotional problems such as anxiety and depression. Some find solace and tranquillity in Buddhism, but others who are under emotional stress sometimes find the unfamiliar atmosphere of a Buddhist meditation hall a frightening experience. For this reason Buddhists sometimes actively discourage such people from taking up Buddhism, although most will try to give them the support they need. Religion is more than therapy; while most religions aim to alleviate human misery in any form, religion is for the healthy as well as the sick. To be medically sound is not necessarily to be spiritually advanced. Buddhism aims at a high spiritual goal which involves one's whole life, and is not just a technique for enabling an anxious student to pass an exam, or for injecting half an hour of calm into an otherwise hectic existence.

Although Buddhism attracts many westerners, the majority of Buddhists in the West are immigrants from Buddhist countries, and it is estimated that there are some 100000 Buddhists in Great Britain, of which at least 20000 are westerners.

Whatever their differences, all Buddhists are familiar with the story of Siddhartha Gautama and how he became the Buddha by gaining enlightenment.

The Story of the Buddha

It was the sixth century BCE when Buddhism began in North India. At that time the *Brahmins* (the highest caste, to which the teacher-priests belong) were studying and teaching scriptures known as the *Vedas* — hymns in praise of the gods — and they performed animal sacrifices on behalf of the other, lower castes. India abounded with sages and scholars, who asked very profound questions about the world and about human existence. Was the world eternal or not? Was the soul distinct from body? What happens to the soul after death?

There was a bewildering variety of religions, but serious seekers were already familiar with ideas which were to become an integral part of Buddhism: *nirvana* (liberation), *yoga* (spiritual path), *samsara* (rebirth), *dharma* (teaching). Even the word *buddha* was already familiar, meaning one who had sought and obtained spiritual awakening. It was in this environment that Siddhartha Gautama, the boy who was to become the Buddha, was born.

What follows is the legend of the Buddha. How much of it is literally true is anyone's guess: we cannot be sure, and, unlike the many Christians who have embarked on the 'quest for the historical Jesus', Buddhists are not particularly interested in discovering how much of the 'storyline' is correct. What the story teaches is more important, and how it can help spiritual progress.

Siddhartha Gautama, it is said, was an Indian prince. Before he was born, his mother, Mahamaya, had a dream: a beautiful white elephant entered her womb through her side. When the brahmin teachers were asked what the dream meant, they replied that she would bear a child who would become either the king of all the world, or else an enlightened sage. Ten lunar months later, she gave birth to a son. When he was five days old, 108 Brahmins were invited to the name-giving ceremony: of these Brahmins, eight were experts at interpreting auspicious marks on a young child's body. Seven of them predicted that if he remained in the palace he would become a world ruler, and that if he left home he would become a buddha. The eighth Brahmin was more definite: Prince Siddhartha was most certainly destined to become a buddha.

Since seven out of the eight Brahmins had predicted two possible destinies for Siddhartha, his father, King Suddhodana was concerned lest the young prince should leave home to take up a religious life. Siddhartha was therefore allowed to enjoy every luxury that the palace could afford, and care was taken that the young prince should not see any sign of suffering or decay. It is even said that when flowers began to wither in the palace they were immediately removed so that Siddhartha would see no sign of unsatisfactoriness.

One day, Siddhartha persuaded his servant Channa to take him on an excursion outside his princely home. This journey proved to be a milestone in his life, for as he and his servant rode they had three encounters: *first*, with an old man; *second*, with a sick man lying by the roadside; and *third* and finally, with a funeral procession. (In funeral processions in India it is customary to carry the corpse exposed, and Siddhartha would therefore have seen the dead body.) Siddhartha had never witnessed anything like this before, and Channa had to explain to him that old age, sickness and death were not only part of human existence, but conditions that Siddhartha himself would experience one day.

All this came as a great shock to Siddhartha. In deep thought he returned homewards, pondering on the nature of human existence which permitted such things. There was a banquet in the palace that night, but Siddhartha refused to attend, preferring to remain in his own room.

The following day, Siddhartha ventured out once more, this time to the market square. There he experienced his *fourth* decisive encounter. There was a wandering holy man, who had renounced the world, begging for food amongst the passers-by. He had no material possessions, and wore nothing but rags; yet he looked serene, as if he had found inner peace. There and then Siddhartha decided that, since he had not experienced inner peace in the palace, he would give up his princely existence, and take up the life of a wandering ascetic.

That night, when the household was asleep, Siddhartha persuaded Channa to mount their horses and ride out of the palace grounds. When they had ridden far into the forest, Siddhartha removed his jewels, exchanged his clothes with Channa, and parted company with him. (Westerners are sometimes shocked that the Buddha-to-be abandoned his wife and child. It is to be remembered that we are in the realms of legend here, not history, and Buddhists with whom I have discussed this point state that he must have discharged his parental responsibilities before his departure. The eastern family unit is a larger one than the western 'nuclear' family, and Siddhartha's family was rich, so he did not leave his wife and child destitute.)

Siddhartha wandered for six years as a religious ascetic. He met five other world-renouncing monks, who recommended severe austerities. According to one version of the legend, Siddhartha ate nothing more than one grain of rice per day! Yet the austere life did not provide Siddhartha with what he was seeking: he still felt that he had not found inner peace. In fact, austerity was beginning to affect the health of these wandering monks: they became as thin as skeletons and could scarcely walk. Siddhartha finally lost consciousness; the other five thought that he was dead, but he revived, and explained that he no longer believed that this was the path to enlightenment.

Siddhartha began to eat again. The other monks accused him of having given up the religious life, and abandoned him. Siddhartha was convinced that the way to gain inner peace was by avoiding extremes: he had experienced a life of luxury in the palace; he had experienced a life of austerity in the forest. Neither had brought the enlightenment which he sought. Siddhartha resolved that, having adopted a 'Middle Way', he would sit under a pipal tree and meditate, not moving from the spot until he had gained enlightenment.

He meditated for seven days, during which he was attacked by Mara (roughly, a Buddhist counterpart to Satan), who employed his armies against Gautama in a futile attempt to distract him from gaining enlightenment. Mara's armies represented the vices of lust, hunger and thirst, craving, sloth, fear, doubt, hypocrisy, hopes of earthly honours, and self-exaltation. However, by his previous existences Gautama had acquired sufficient virtues to withstand such temptations, and he continued in meditation until he had reached *nirvana* (enlightenment).

Gautama gained many startling insights during this period of meditation. He received knowledge of all his former existences. (It is to be remembered that Buddhists hold that one is reborn many times before gaining enlightenment.) Some 530 previous lives are recorded: 24 times as a prince, 85 times a king, 22 times a scholar, 42 times a god, twice a thief, once a slave and many times a lion, a horse, an eagle and a snake. The stories of the previous lives of the Buddha are collected in popular folk tales known as the *jatakas*.

The Hare in the Moon

The *jatakas* enshrine simple moral and religious messages, such as the importance of fulfilling one's obligations, or the triumph of good over evil. One well loved *jataka* is the story of the Hare in the Moon. The Buddha-to-be was reborn as a hare, and had three special friends — a monkey, a jackal and an otter. The hare preached to his friends about the importance of almsgiving, keeping the precepts, and observing the days of fasting when one should give food to beggars. A fastday was approaching: the otter found some fish, the jackal a broiled lizard, and the monkey some bunches of mangoes. When the hare found some grass, he realised that although hares could eat it, one could hardly offer grass to a beggar. After careful thought, the hare decided what to do: instead of offering a beggar grass, he would offer his own body for the beggar to eat.

The mighty god Indra knew the hare's thought, and decided to test his sincerity. He disguised himself as a beggar, and went to the four animals. The otter offered fish, the jackal his broiled lizard and the monkey gave him mangoes. When the beggar reached the hare, the hare instructed him to prepare a fire on which he, the hare, would cook himself. Being a god, Indra miraculously conjured up a fire, on to which the hare then jumped. Because Indra had proved the hare's sincerity, he also ensured that the fire would not burn him.

In order to remind humankind of the Buddha-hare's deed, Indra etched on the surface of the moon the figure of a hare. (This is why many Buddhists claim to see the contours of the moon as a hare, and not as the 'man in the moon' which westerners imagine.) The otter, jackal and monkey attained good rebirths for their generosity to Indra.

The 'moral' of the story is straightforward: fulfilling one's religious obligations brings merit, and ideally one should practise compassion and generosity even to the point of self-sacrifice.

Buddhism and the Gods

The *jatakas* also relate that the Buddha had 42 previous births as a god. It is therefore inaccurate to claim that Buddhism is an atheistic religion. Buddhists are prepared to believe that there may be gods, and that these gods might offer help with the problems of daily living: for example, if a farmer wants a good harvest or if a student wants to pass an examination. Buddhist lay persons will sometimes pray to gods for these benefits, but this kind of prayer, although not discouraged, is not part of the Buddhist faith. Buddhists do not hold that there is one supreme God who has created and who sustains the world. Finally, the gods themselves are impermanent. Although their existence is pleasant, it will come to an end, just as our human existences will end, and the gods, like humans and animals, are subject to *samsara* — rebirth.

Another insight which Siddhartha gained under the pipal tree was knowledge of what caused living beings to be born and reborn. It was because they were essentially ignorant of the laws which governed the world. As long as they remain ignorant, they will reap the effects of their deeds. This law is called the law of *karma*. Karma means 'deeds' and the law of karma states that every deed has an effect on our pleasure or pain, either in this life or in a life which is still to come. Once a living being sees how things really are, and how he or she is bound to this seemingly endless cycle of birth and rebirth (samsara), it becomes obvious that it is selfish desire which ties us to the wheel of samsara. Once ignorance and selfish desire are removed, by following the 'Middle Way', Siddhartha gained the inner peace which he had sought. From that time on, Siddhartha Gautama was the enlightened one — the Buddha. (*Buddha* means 'enlightened' or 'awakened'.) 'Buddha' is therefore a title, not a name, just as 'Christ' is a title, not a name. Of course there are important differences. The Buddha was a man, not a god or a divine messenger or saviour. The Buddha was not unique, but is an example for others to follow. In theory, at least, all Buddhists are trying to reach this enlightened state — nirvana — although very few actually achieve it in practice during their present lifetime.

The Buddha begins to Teach

After Siddhartha Gautama — now the Buddha — had attained nirvana, he met the five wandering ascetics again. They recognised that he had gained the inner peace which he was seeking and they asked him to explain what he had discovered. The Buddha preached his first sermon to them, near the town of Benares (now called Varanasi). In this sermon he explained the doctrine of the 'Middle Way' — the avoidance of excesses of wealth and poverty — and also what are known as the Four Noble Truths and the Eightfold Path. Although there are many types of Buddhism, and many schools of thought, all Buddhists would accept the Noble Truths and endeavour to follow the Path which the Buddha taught.

The Noble Truths are as follows:

1   The existence of unsatisfactoriness.
2   The cause of unsatisfactoriness.
3   The elimination of unsatisfactoriness.
4   The path to the elimination of unsatisfactoriness.

I have chosen the word 'unsatisfactoriness', clumsy though it is, since I believe it is the English word which translates most effectively the otherwise untranslatable word *dukkha*. Most writers on Buddhism use the word 'suffering' or — worse still — 'pain'. This not only gives the totally wrong impression that Buddhists are miserable people, but also describes only a part of dukkha. Dukkha occurs even when we are enjoying ourselves: for example, a high-spirited party is dukkha, because it falls short of what we should truly be seeking. It should also be noted that, although it is only living beings that can suffer or feel pain, *all* the universe is unsatisfactory. For example, this book is 'unsatisfactory', although clearly it cannot literally 'suffer'. It is unsatisfactory for various reasons: it does not have any colour illustrations, there is better quality paper on which it could have been printed, it depends on many factors for its continued existence (such as human care), and one day it will disintegrate or be destroyed.

The Buddha presented the Four Noble Truths just as a medical doctor of his time pronounced a diagnosis at a consultation. A doctor in sixth century India would first of all identify the illness (let us say, dysentery); he would next state its cause (contaminated food); then he would reassure the patient that the disease could be cured (the elimination of dysentery); finally he would prescribe the cure (possibly a liquid diet and a suitable medicine). The Buddha was therefore a kind of 'spiritual doctor', someone who was able to diagnose what was wrong with the human condition and to prescribe a suitable remedy. The remedy is to be found in the Eightfold Path, which consists of:

1 Perfect view.
2 Perfect aspiration.
3 Perfect speech.
4 Perfect conduct.
5 Perfect livelihood.
6 Perfect effort.
7 Perfect mindfulness.
8 Perfect absorption.

I have deliberately chosen the adjective 'perfect' instead

of 'right'. (Both translations are equally possible.) This is because expressions like 'right view' often convey to westerners the idea of getting one's facts right. To have 'perfect view', however, does not mean that there is a special creed which one is now able to believe; it is a matter of experiencing the truth rather than merely placing it in one's mental filing cabinet.

Some comment on certain aspects of the Path is necessary. 'Perfect view' refers us back to the Four Noble Truths. 'Perfect speech' means more than simply telling the truth; it entails the avoidance of harsh speech, unprofitable speech and idle gossip. Sometimes spreading truths about people can be more damaging than spreading untruths. 'Perfect livelihood' means making one's living in an honest and moral way; it would be considered wrong to earn one's living by manufacturing armaments or dealing with alcohol. 'Perfect effort' has a much more precise meaning than 'trying hard': it means that one must take appropriate steps to prevent the causes for selfish desires arising. (One must avoid being tempted, not simply overcome temptation.) The sixth step therefore refers to the meditative practices, which are points seven and eight, and which will be revisited in a later chapter. The last is impossible to translate: essentially *samadhi* means the ideal result of meditation, the most important function of which is to recognise in a deep inner experience that there is no self. This is by no means easy subject-matter to digest, and it takes us on to Buddhist doctrines, which will also be explored later.

The Results of the Benares Sermon

After listening to the Buddha, the five monks embraced his teaching, and decided to follow Gautama's invitation to join him in forming a community of disciples. Thus, the first *Sangha* (community of monks) was formed. As the Buddha continued to preach, many more were added to the Sangha and to the ever-increasing numbers of lay followers. Many who came to heckle or confront the Buddha found themselves converted to Buddhism — even notorious criminals. Some people attributed the success of his preaching to miraculous powers, and there are many stories of the Buddha performing miraculous cures.

The Buddha had a message for society too. His followers rejected the Vedic scriptures and refused to take part in the animal sacrifices carried out by the Brahmin priests. They did not worship the Vedic gods, since they did not believe that worshipping the gods would bring one any nearer to nirvana. In addition, the Buddha taught that the class divisions of his society were far less important than distinctions between good and evil people. The true Brahmin was not the one who carried out the prescribed religious ceremonies, but the one who did good, avoided evil and had a pure heart.

The Message Spreads

For 45 years the Buddha travelled the length and breadth of North India, proclaiming these teachings, and attracting an ever-increasing number of followers. The Buddha's father heard of the enthusiasm which attended the teachings of the Buddha and his disciples, and he invited members of the Sangha to Kapilavastu, his home town. Instead of staying at the royal palace which he had abandoned many years before, the Buddha and his followers wandered from house to house doing their alms-round to obtain food. At first King Suddhodana was offended, but when he learned that this was their normal practice he accepted their custom, and undertook to provide one meal for the Sangha at his royal court. As a consequence, many members of the Buddha's family became his followers, including his former wife Yasodhara, his son Rahula, and the king himself.

When the Buddha was 80 years old he became unwell at the beginning of the rainy season. At one of his meals he inadvertently ate some contaminated food, and died after contracting dysentery. As he lay on his death-bed in a grove, he gave some final instructions to Ananda, his closest follower. His instructions were that his followers should find liberation for themselves and not simply accept his teaching on authority, but test it out in their own experience. This does not mean of course that followers of the Buddha should devise any old set of teachings and practices they choose: a seeker must follow the Eightfold Path and the Precepts for a substantial period before that person is in a position to decide whether the Buddha's teaching is true.

The death of the Buddha is called his *parinirvana*. Death after reaching nirvana means that one never again returns to the realm of samsara (rebirth). This was the Buddha's first pronouncement after attaining nirvana; it is recorded in a famous Buddhist scripture called the *Dhammapada*, and is sometimes called the Buddha's 'Song of Victory':

> Through many a birth in samsara have I wandered in vain, seeking the builder of this house [of life]. Repeated birth is indeed suffering!
> O house-builder, you are seen! You will not build this house again. For your rafters are broken and your ridge-pole shattered. My mind has reached the Unconditioned: I have attained the destruction of craving.[1]

The 'house' is the life into which one is reborn, the house-builder is desire, and the ridge-pole is ignorance. Since the Buddha had eliminated his selfish desire and ignorance, they could no longer create and sustain a new 'house'.

Some religious founders have appointed successors to lead the community of followers. The Buddha did not do this, but stated that he was to be succeeded by the *Dharma* (the law, or teaching) and the Sangha (the community of followers). The Buddha, Dharma and Sangha are sometimes known as the 'three gems' or 'three jewels' of Buddhism, and it is not uncommon to see the sign of the triple gem portrayed in Buddhist art.

Although the Dharma was declared to be one of the Buddha's successors, the Buddha did not leave any written teachings. After his death, the monks convened the First Buddhist Council at Rajgir in North India, at which they recited the teachings which they faithfully remembered, and agreed upon them. It was several centuries before these teachings were finally written down: the first known collection of written teachings was made in Sri Lanka in the first century BCE.

These teachings are known variously as the 'Pali canon' (the scriptures were originally written in a language similar to Pali, and 'canon' means 'norm' or 'standard'), or the *Tipitaka*, meaning, literally, 'triple basket'. The reason for the latter rather curious name is that the Pali scriptures fell into three broad sections: there were disciplinary rules for the monks (the *Vinaya-pitaka*), statements of teachings or doctrines (*Sutta-pitaka*), and later elaborations (*Abhidhamma-pitaka*), mainly teachings about the human mind.

The language of the early Buddhist scriptures contrasted with that of the Brahmins, who used Sanskrit. Although it might have seemed an advantage to have Buddhist scriptures in the common language, Sanskrit was the 'prestige' language used by the Brahmins, in much the same way as Latin was the 'prestige' language of the Christian Church until modern times. As a result, Buddhism was failing to attract the Brahmins, who were already opposed to Buddhism since their caste status was being threatened by the Buddhists' disregard for caste. Religions are seldom popular with those whose vested interests are threatened by them.

Note to Chapter 1

1 Acharya Buddharakkhita (translator), *The Dhammapada* (Buddhist Publication Society, Kandy, Sri Lanka, 1985) vv 152–153

2

Thervada and Mahayana Buddhists

Westerners who take the trouble to find out about Buddhism can become acquainted with most, if not all, of its varieties. It is therefore possible as an outsider to become more familiar with the spectrum of Buddhist traditions than many 'insiders'. Many lay Buddhists in, let us say, Burma, will be vaguely aware that their tradition of Buddhism is not the only one, but, if they were asked to explain the differences between Theravada and Mahayana Buddhism, they would be quite unable to do so. This is not to discredit Buddhists: after all, how many members of the British established Churches could give an account of Greek Orthodoxy — or vice versa? In this chapter we shall look at the main differences between the two main forms of Buddhism — Theravada and Mahayana — and how this split arose.

Religion is a controversial subject, and every religion has to devise a method for dealing with divisions which arise. Buddhism's attitude to disagreements is interesting. As we saw, the Buddha never insisted that enquirers should agree with his teaching. Only if their experience confirmed what he taught, should they follow him. If it did not, then they should follow what their experience dictated.

Buddhists sometimes actively discourage seekers from converting to Buddhism, if it seems that they would fare better by following some other path. Since one has many lives to live and not just one, it is possible that someone might make more spiritual progress through, say, Christianity than through Buddhism; perhaps in some future existence that person will be drawn towards Buddhism and eventually obtain enlightenment. The Buddhist path is not to be hurried.

There is also no pressure for all Buddhists to agree with one another. Indeed, splits have never been caused in Buddhism because monks have disagreed on points of doctrine: no one can be expelled from the Sangha for holding unorthodox beliefs. What cannot exist in harmony, however, are different groups of monks who engage in conflicting religious practices. This disrupts monastic life, and disrupting the Sangha is a very serious offence. A monk who cannot accept the rules of his order has only two options: he must either conform or leave.

The 'Greater Sangha Party'

As Buddhism developed, it was perhaps inevitable that disagreements occurred, and so two main traditions emerged. These are the 'Hinayana' which is said to survive in the Theravada tradition today, and the Mahayana traditions. Although there are significant differences between them, the origins of the split between the two are shrouded in mystery, and it is far from clear which Buddhists disagreed with whom, and for what reasons. However, we do know that there were two principal events which heralded the split.

First, a group of monks in the Vajji territory (near the Nepalese border, north-west of Patna) were alleged to be breaking the rules of the *Vinaya* (the scriptures which set the rules for the monastic community). They were accused of eating after mid-day, of storing salt in horns (allegedly contravening a precept forbidding monks to store food), and handling money. It was not so much a problem that rules laid down by the Buddha were being infringed. During his lifetime, the Buddha had taught that changes in monastic rules were permissible, but with one proviso: the entire Sangha must agree. In this instance, it could not. These monks were taken to task by the other Buddhist communities and a Second Buddhist Council was called to consider the situation. A working party of four monks was appointed to look into the problem, and these monks reported to the Council that the behaviour of the monks at Vajji was unlawful.

The Council accepted this decision. The dissenting monks, however, did not. They set themselves up as a community in its own right — a gross misdeed according to Buddhist teaching. Causing a schism in the Sangha is a cardinal offence. However, they had sown the seeds for questioning and developing traditional ideas within Buddhism. According to the Theravadin account, this dissenting group became the *Mahasanghika* — the 'Greater Sangha Party' — from which Mahayana Buddhism was born.

Other Buddhists find difficulty with this account. The name 'Greater Sangha Party' suggests a majority of Buddhists, yet the monks of Vajji were a minority who were overruled. It has therefore been suggested that the rise of the Mahayana tradition stemmed from another dispute altogether.

This *second* dispute involved a monk called Mahadeva, some 40 or 50 years after the earlier incident. Previously, it was believed that an *arhat* (an enlightened one) was perfect: he committed no misdeeds, and was completely all-knowing. Mahadeva questioned this. Some *arhats*, he said, were ignorant: he had sometimes seen them lose their way on their travels. They were prone to human weaknesses too, he claimed, since many of them had erotic dreams at night! Mahadeva suggested that existing Buddhist teachings were incomplete and he wanted to introduce new material. He also recommended rather unusual means of entering the path towards enlightenment, such as following 'vocal sounds'. (It is unclear what he meant by this.)

This caused the Sangha to examine the status of the *arhat*. Was he so perfect after all? Was there perhaps some further goal beyond the *arhat* which Buddhists ought to seek? Should not Buddhists strive to become fully complete perfect buddhas instead? These questions demanded serious reflection, and some members of the Sangha developed new teachings in order to solve these problems. Those who believe that Mahadeva heralded Mahayana Buddhism claim that he and his followers represented the majority of Buddhist opinion. Those monks who could not agree with him separated themselves from this majority and in time became known as 'Hinayana' Buddhists.

'Mahayana' means 'greater vehicle', and 'Hinayana' means 'lesser vehicle'. Although Mahayana Buddhists are happy to be described as such, it is understandable that the more conservative Buddhist is unhappy with the description 'Hinayana': no one wants to admit that he or she is journeying in the 'lesser vehicle'! Buddhists today who do not belong to the Mahayana tradition prefer the term 'Theravada', meaning 'doctrine of the elders'.

In response to the questions which caused the controversy, the Mahayana tradition claimed that a buddha was more than a human being, but was a super-human figure; he did not merely have wisdom, which the *arhats* were supposed to possess, but combined the ideal of wisdom with compassion. This latter ideal enabled Mahayana Buddhism to give greater attention to the religious hopes of the laity. The laity had shown loving kindness by providing material support for the Sangha, so it therefore seemed right that they too should be able to make progress along the Buddhist path.

Examining the evidence

The second explanation of the split between the two traditions has its problems too. In theory, differences of belief ought not to divide the Sangha: what holds the Sangha together is its uniformity in practice. Practice is always considered to be more important than doctrine, and Theravadin monks to whom I have spoken certainly do not think it important to consider whether *arhats* can be ignorant or have erotic dreams. Yet the dispute between the two main Buddhist traditions seems to have been about doctrines, not practices. So what really happened?

One possibility is that, when Buddhists debated these issues, some groups of monks tended to favour one set of opinions and other groups a different set. As time progressed, monks would gravitate towards communities which accepted teachings with which they felt most at home.

One might compare this with what happens in Christian Churches: 'fundamentalists' and 'liberals' have not formed separate denominations, yet some churches gain a reputation for attracting the fundamentalists and others the more liberal believers. This may well have happened in the early stages of Buddhism, the only difference being that the two traditions finally did separate from each other. It is possible that, as the two traditions developed, so did distinctive monastic and ritual practices: once this happened, monks from one tradition could no longer live comfortably within a Sangha which followed another tradition.

One further point is worth mentioning about the two forms of Buddhism. It is often said that Theravada Buddhism is more 'orthodox' and closer to the teachings of Gautama the Buddha. Many Mahayana Buddhists would question this claim. Indeed, there is a story that at the First Buddhist Council at Rajgir, when all the monks had recited and agreed on the Buddha's teachings, another monk arrived late. When he heard what had been decided, he replied, 'Well, I prefer to accept the Buddha's teachings as I remember them'. If the story is true, it shows that even at a fairly early stage different accounts of the Buddha's teachings were circulating, and that the members of the First Buddhist Council did not necessarily reflect what the Buddha himself taught.

The 'Three Bodies' of the Buddha

We must now look at how these two notions — the supermundane Buddha, and the ideal of compassion — which have been taught in the Mahayana tradition. (The material about the Buddha's 'three bodies' may not be easy to understand, and readers who are less interested in Buddhist doctrines can comfortably skip this section.)

Traditionally, Buddhism has been a religion of self-effort; a 'do-it-yourself' religion, as I have heard some Buddhists say. The *Dhammapada* states: 'You yourselves must strive; the Buddhas only point the way.'[1]

Buddhism is unusual in this respect. Religions generally

offer supernatural aid or support to the follower. It was perhaps inevitable, then, that the notion of supernatural help should find its way into Buddhism.

There is another factor which made the introduction of supernatural aid a logical development within Buddhism. Particularly in the West, Buddhism has been accused of being a selfish religion. On the surface, it looks as if individuals must follow the Buddhist path by their own efforts to gain personal enlightenment, not the enlightenment of others. So it is easily assumed that the Buddhist must make spiritual progress alone, being unable to help or receive help from anyone else.

This view of Buddhism is unfair. All traditions insist that the Buddha taught his followers about the importance of compassion as well as gaining the clear insight which removes ignorance. If compassion is so important, then could it be true that a Buddha, once deceased, was 'beyond recall', having no further contact with men and women who were struggling within the constant cycle of birth and rebirth?

Accordingly, a Mahayana teaching developed that the Buddha was not 'beyond recall', but continued to live in a celestial realm, after (and also before) his appearance as a historical figure on the earth. This celestial Buddha is a spiritual body known as a 'bliss-body' or 'enjoyment-body' (*samboghakaya*). With this body, he continued to give teachings in the celestial realm — to celestial monks, to enlightened ones (*arhats*) and to *bodhisattvas* (see the next section) — which could be passed on to humans when they were ready for them. His followers were urged not just to become enlightened beings who had discovered their own path to liberation, but complete buddhas who existed beyond the human realm, and who could continue to offer spiritual aid to other living beings. Gautama, the historical Buddha, had a physical body which was conjured up (*nirmanakaya*) by the spiritual celestial Buddha as a skilful means of teaching humankind the Dharma.

There is a further dimension to this line of thought. Mahayana Buddhism teaches that there can be many Buddhas in each age, and not merely one at a time, as the Theravadins hold. We have already seen that for the Buddhist there are no souls, and that there is no permanent being inside each one of us, enabling me to say that this body is 'mine' or another person's body is 'yours'. Strictly speaking, then, there is no real distinction between me, the author, and you, the reader. Likewise there is no real distinction between Gautama the historical Buddha, Dipankara (an earlier Buddha), Maitreya (the Buddha of the next age), Amitabha (the Buddha of infinite light), and so on. Ultimately, these beings are one and the same, sharing the same 'absolute body' or 'truth-body' (the *dharmakaya*).

Compassion and the Bodhisattva

Since it is important not to slip away into nirvana, but to help other living beings, Mahayana Buddhism developed a further ideal beyond seeking personal enlightenment. One should not strive for one's own nirvana, but for the liberation of all living beings from the cycle of birth and rebirth. So with Mahayana Buddhism came the concept of the *bodhisattva*. The *bodhisattva* is one who has attained all the perfections, and gained enlightenment, but, in order to help living beings, does not enter a nirvana which is 'beyond recall'. The help which the *bodhisattva* offers has sometimes been compared with 'divine grace', but of course that is a Christian term and not a Buddhist one. The term the Buddhist would prefer to use is 'transference of merit': the *bodhisattva* has acquired more merit than he (or she) needs, and can pass on this additional merit to those who call upon him. When a *bodhisattva* comes to earth to take on a physical body, such an action is not 'rebirth' in the same way as humans and animals are reborn. The *bodhisattva* chooses to take on a body: he is not caused to do so as a consequence of deeds, for he has acquired infinitely more merit than he needs to escape the cycle of birth and rebirth.

The *bodhisattva* can offer physical or spiritual help to humankind. There are stories of *bodhisattvas* assuming a physical body, and then sacrificing it to feed hungry animals.

At other times, a *bodhisattva* can offer spiritual guidance to the follower by showing the appropriate path to nirvana. The best known of the *bodhisattvas* is one with the rather formidable name of Avalokiteshvara. Avalokiteshvara, the story goes, was about to enter into nirvana when he heard a cry for help. The cry, which came from the human realm, grew louder, and was joined by other human cries. Avalokiteshvara found himself unable to slip into nirvana while there remained so much suffering to be alleviated. The name 'Avalokiteshvara' means 'the lord who looked down'; Avalokiteshvara looks down on the unsatisfactoriness of the world and offers his help to those who call upon him.

The Spread of Buddhism

These then are some of the main differences between Theravada and Mahayana Buddhism. The two traditions spread in different directions, Theravada Buddhism spreading south and Mahayana north. Because Mahayana Buddhists interpreted monastic rules more liberally than the Theravadin orders, they were able to adapt better to the colder climates of the Himalayas. They were more flexible, too, in accommodating the beliefs and practices of other religions which they met, such as Shamanism in Tibet and Taoism in China. Mahayana Buddhism was brought to Nepal, and through the Himalayas to Tibet, Mongolia, China, Korea and Japan. The Theravada tradition spread to Sri Lanka, Burma and Thailand. The two traditions are sometimes known, therefore, as the 'northern' and the 'southern' traditions.

Although Buddhism travelled north and south of India, and indeed right through it, as it spread, there is little that remains of Buddhism in India today. It is now only found to any significant degree in Kashmir and Himachal Pradesh, in the north-west. The caste system and the strength of the prevailing Hindu faiths proved too strong for Buddhism. Although Buddhism was opposed to caste, it never succeeded in abolishing it, and the Indian people found great conflict between their social conventions and the Buddhist religion which rejected them.

The Indian people were also unwilling to abandon their gods. In theory, this was no problem for Buddhism, in which it is perfectly permissible to pay homage to the gods and also follow the Buddhist path; however, financially the people could not afford to look after their Hindu temples and maintain a Sangha too. A Hindu tradition arose that the great god Vishnu took on the physical form of the Buddha, and this legend in effect led to the Buddha becoming part of Hinduism.

Although the traditional Buddhist sites at Bodh Gaya and Sarnath (near Varanasi) are well supported and are endowed with many Buddhist temples, these are often places of pilgrimage for Hindus as well, who revere the Buddha as an incarnation of Vishnu. Pilgrims go to the shrines (and even to the nearby archaeological museum at Bodh Gaya) and place small coins in the hands of the Buddha-images. Attaching gold leaf to a statue is believed to bring merit, and the less affluent who cannot themselves afford gold leaf will touch the gold embellishments and then their foreheads as a token of devotion.

The Muslim invasions of India from the eleventh century onwards struck a fatal blow to Buddhism: Buddhism once had support from previous Indian rulers, but had now lost its royal patronage. Yet, despite its decline in the country where the Buddha first preached, Buddhism continues elsewhere to thrive in both its southern and northern forms.

The Cult of Ambedkar

Although Buddhism now only has a following in India of around three million amidst a 700 million population, the Buddhist path offers one important advantage at least to Hindus of lower caste: Buddhism rejects the caste system, and consequently some recent attempt at reintroducing Buddhism has been possible. This has been spearheaded by a Dr Bhimrao Ramji Ambedkar (1891–1956), who was born an untouchable. His family belonged to a Hindu Reform Movement, and as a result he had the good fortune to receive a high school and college education at Columbia University, New York, where he studied law and gained a PhD. Returning to India, he took up the causes of the untouchables.

Mahatma Gandhi, statesman, social reformer and Hindu leader, had already taken up the cause of the untouchables, but Ambedkar went further than Gandhi. Gandhi had opposed the continued existence of the outcastes, who were outwith the caste system. However, Gandhi still believed that the caste system itself served a useful function in maintaining social order. Ambedkar did not agree: 'Nothing can emancipate the outcaste except the destruction of the caste system,' he insisted. In 1936 Ambedkar founded the Independent Labour Party, and became Minister of Law in 1937. He secured some privileges for the 'outcastes' in education and in government service.

Converting to another religion did not secure unmitigated blessings for the Hindu. Members of recognised castes had certain legal privileges which were denied to those who converted to another faith. Ambedkar, however, believed that as long as he remained a Hindu there would always be an obstacle to equality and emancipation. In 1935 he expressed an intention to convert to another religion, but it was not until 1950 that he finally decided to convert to Buddhism, and called upon the rest of the untouchable community to accept it. On the 14 October 1956 he was initiated as a Buddhist: this was the last year of his life — he died on 6 December 1956.

Notwithstanding Ambedkar's short official recognition as a Buddhist, he is regarded as a *bodhisattva* today, and is even taken as a Fourth Refuge. Followers of Ambedkar, when taking refuge, will say:

> I take the Buddha as my refuge.
> I take the Dharma as my refuge.
> I take the Sangha as my refuge.
> I take Ambedkar as my refuge.

Note to Chapter 2

1   Acharya Buddharakkhita (translator), *The Dhammapada*, v 276

3

Buddhist Teachings

Of all religions, Christianity has felt most acutely the need for its followers — particularly its clergy — to accept a set of agreed orthodox doctrines. By contrast, Buddhism, in common with a number of other religions, often claims to be a 'religion without dogma'. In claiming this, Buddhists mean that it is more important to practise the Dharma than to believe a set of truths set out in a creed. Nevertheless, Buddhism has produced many scholars and developed some very elaborate teachings.

The Buddha's first sermon at Benares contained not merely the Four Noble Truths and the Eightfold Path, but many basic teachings which were almost immediately regarded as central to the Buddhist faith. This chapter explores some of the teachings which stem from the 'perfect view' expounded by the Buddha. Although we will confine ourselves to the basics and not the complexities of Buddhist philosophy, this material may still prove much more difficult to assimilate than preceding and subsequent chapters. Readers who believe in 'skipping' chapters may therefore proceed directly to Chapter Four. I have included this material, partly because some will find it of interest, but also because we would not do justice to Buddhism if we ignored its teachings, scholars and thinkers.

The Three Marks of Existence

In the Benares sermon, preached to the five monks, the Buddha taught that there are three important Marks of Existence (often called 'signs of being' in English). They are:

36

1 *Dukkha*: unsatisfactoriness.
2 *Anicca*: impermanence.
3 *Anatta*: literally, 'non-self'.

We have already described *dukkha* (unsatisfactoriness), which pervades all of existence. All is *dukkha* because everything is impermanent (*anicca*). As the well-known Christian hymn, 'Abide with me', puts it, 'Change and decay in all around I see'. Objects change: the car I purchased a few years ago has begun to decay with rust, its colour has faded, its upholstery is worn. People change: a lover may find that love has become cold, or we may have trusted someone implicitly and found one day that our trust was misplaced. Medically speaking, our cells are changing all the time: they die and (for the most part) replace themselves; since no one's body possesses a single cell that existed seven years ago, in a sense I am not the same person as I was in the year 1981. The only state which is unchanging is nirvana: enlightenment. Once a being is enlightened, there is no falling back into the cycle of birth and rebirth.

This brings us to the doctrine of *anatta*, the 'non-self'. With a few minor exceptions, Buddhists have taught that the 'self' is unreal: there is no enduring soul which will survive death, or enter nirvana. Equally there is no 'world-soul' or creator God who sustains the universe. The doctrine of the 'non-self' is not easy to understand. An early Buddhist king called Milinda once demanded an explanation from a monk called Nagasena. Nagasena explained this teaching by comparing the 'self' with a chariot. What is it that makes a chariot a chariot? The wheels are not the chariot; the axle is not the chariot; the frame is not the chariot; the yoke that ties the chariot to the horse is not the chariot. Yet when we have listed all the parts of the chariot, we do not find a further thing called 'chariot-ness' (if one may put it so), which really makes the chariot the chariot. Once we have itemised the parts, there is nothing more. Thus it is with the self· I am not the same as my hair, my arms, my legs, or any of my organs; yet, Nagasena explained to the king, there is no 'self' which exists over and above the physical parts of which I am composed.

It is not enough to be convinced in our minds that this teaching is true: we must experience *anatta* too. We are usually unable to do this because we are so possessive by nature, insisting, 'This is mine!' or complaining, 'I don't like this,' or 'I hurt myself'. According to Buddhist teaching, we suffer from 'Three Fires' — ignorance, greed and hatred. It is easy to see greed and hatred as 'fires' which we can fuel; yet although ignorance is not so obviously a fiery element within us, ignorance lies at the root of all humankind's problems, because it gives us the sense of 'I', which we take to be so important. It is ignorance which makes us think that there is some permanent substance or soul which lies inside our 'body, feelings, sensations, "mental formations", and consciousness'. (The five items just listed are known as the 'Five Aggregates' or 'Five Heaps' which make up our personality.)

Rebirth without Selves?

It is because there is no real enduring self that Buddhists prefer to talk about 'rebirth' rather than 'reincarnation', for there is no soul which transmigrates from one existence to the next. This presents us with an obvious problem. If Buddhism holds that there are no such things as 'selves', how can future existences be caused by 'myself'; and, if there is no real, permanent, enduring self, what is it that is reborn?

Strictly speaking, nothing at all carries over from one existence to the next. The explanation is something like this. Let us take the example of the author, conventionally known as 'George Chryssides'. According to the Buddhist, I have no eternal soul, but, because my behaviour in this life has left a lot to be desired, I have 'generated *karma*' because of my past actions. Therefore, unless I gain enlightenment (which is improbable), my *karma* will cause a further being to be born after I die. It is unlikely that this new being would be called 'George Chryssides' — a most surprising coincidence! In all probability, this being would not look like me or act like me, and indeed he or she may not even be a human being.

So there is both a continuity and a discontinuity between

this life and the next: existence in 'my' next life is a result of deeds done in this life, but the being who is born is neither the same nor different. Buddhists often make a comparison with a candle flame. One candle flame can light another candle: the flame is passed on and the second flame can outlast the blowing out of the first. The first flame causes the second, but it would be senseless to say that the two flames were one and the same, and there is certainly no substance called 'fire' or 'flame' which passes from one candle to the next.

This train of thought leads on to another important Buddhist teaching. It has a rather forbidding name — Dependent Origination. It is presented in the form of a list, as indeed many Buddhist teachings are. Buddhism is very fond of numbered lists: we have already encountered the Four Noble Truths, the Eightfold Path, the three Marks of Existence, the Three Fires, and the Five Aggregates, and there are several more lists still to come. The list runs as follows:

Past life:
1   Ignorance.
2   Karma formations.
3   Consciousness.
4   Name and form.
5   The six senses.[1]

Present life:
6   Sense-feeling.
7   Feeling.
8   Craving.
9   Grasping.
10 Becoming.

Future life:
11 Birth.
12 Old age and death.

The simplest way to think of it is to imagine a row of candles, where only the first is lit. The first candle is then used to light the second, the second to light the third, and so on. By the time the last candle is lit, let us imagine that the first candle that has gone out needs to be rekindled by the last. Each stage on the list is like the candle flame which kindles the next.

It is not part of the Buddhist belief that there is a supply of bodies which awaits the arrival of the appropriate *karma*: it is one's *karma* which creates the mind and the body of the living being which takes its birth. The chain of Dependent Origination then continues in motion, and comes round in a full circle. After death, ignorance and karma-formations will give rise to consciousness, and so it goes on. The chain is called 'Dependent Origination' because each link *depends* on the previous one. But each stage does not follow inevitably: it is possible to break the link, by removing ignorance or selfish desire (craving).

The comparison with the candle has often made Westerners think that nirvana is the blowing out of the candle, the extinction of the self. But this is quite wrong. One cannot extinguish the self if there is no self to extinguish. What is extinguished in nirvana is the ignorance which results in selfish desire. When selfish desire, the cause of unsatisfactoriness, is eliminated, then nirvana is attained, and one is never again reborn. It seems strange that the extinction of desire should be confused with the extinction of the self. If I have a tremendous thirst and quench it by having a drink, no one would suppose that I had extinguished myself as well as the thirst! Yet similarly muddled thinking takes place when it is supposed that because nirvana is the end of thirsting after material things, that it is the end of the (non-existent) self which thirsts for them.

'Karma' and Rebirth

In common with Hinduism Buddhism teaches that there are many lives before reaching nirvana. We have the fortune of having been born human in this birth, and a Buddhist regards this as a great and possibly rare opportunity. It is only as a human being that one has the opportunity to hear the *Dharma* (teaching), and to advance on one's spiritual path. In particular, it is only as a human being that one can pursue the monastic life which, at least in the Theravada tradition, is normally regarded as a necessary step in the attainment of enlightenment.

We have seen that we are reborn as a result of our deeds. To follow the Eightfold Path, to observe the Precepts, to perform acts of devotion, or to lend support to the Sangha will all earn merit to secure a favourable rebirth. To act wrongly — for example, by killing, stealing, or slandering — is to store up conditions which will result in a less desirable existence. That we are born according to our deeds is a fixed and unalterable law of the universe, and it is known as the law of *karma*.

The law of *karma* is not a divine punishment. There is no celestial being who judges us according to what we have done. *Karma* is a law that operates in the world quite independently of the wills of people or of gods. Just as the law of gravity entails that a weight will fall if it is dropped from a height, so the law of *karma* entails that one continually will be born and reborn in accordance with one's actions. The only difference between the law of gravity and the law of *karma* is that the former is a physical law, while the latter is a spiritual law; but common to both is the fact that they cannot be defied — just as I cannot decide to remain suspended in mid-air if my parachute will not open, I cannot secure myself a good rebirth if my actions do not merit it.

The law of *karma* provides an explanation for the inequalities and the sufferings of human and animal life. It also helps to explain why some people are born with particular skills and talents; for example, the infant prodigy may have learned his or her skills in a previous birth. Human experiences which are otherwise difficult to account for find a ready explanation in the law of *karma*: a child who dies young may once have been a murderer of a child, who now experiences the appropriate result of that misdeed.

Although the effects of one's actions will be reaped in time, the catching-up is not always immediate. It may take several successive existences to burn out all the effects of actions committed within one single existence. What I am experiencing in this life, for example, may therefore be the consequence not of my immediate past life, but of existences lived several lives ago. Although someone may sometimes seem to escape from the consequences of actions, ultimately no escape is possible. If I should be foolish enough to think that suicide might prevent me from reaping the results of previous misdeeds, I must realise that the suicide will be reborn somewhere else in the universe — perhaps as a ghost or in one of the hells. I can end this present life, but I cannot stop living in some form or other; and, of course, since suicide is itself a misdeed, the act of taking my own life would itself accrue bad *karma* which must work itself out in the form of suffering.

It is sometimes suggested that belief in *karma* makes Buddhists (and Hindus too) complacent about their lot in life. Why should a sick person seek a cure if the illness is due to previous misdeeds? Since one cannot ultimately escape from the effects of one's deeds, will not the law of *karma* catch up at some later stage with someone who recovers? In answer to this question, the Buddha listed altogether four causes of illness. *Karma* is one cause, but the weather, food, and faulty posture are three others: getting soaked through may cause a chill; poisoned food may cause dysentery; a faulty gait may cause curvature of the spine. So the law of karma is only one of several natural laws which govern the universe. There are, in sum, five natural laws:

1   the order of seasons;
2   the germination of seeds;
3   the laws governing mental activities;
4   karma; and
5   other laws which we cannot explain any further — such as the law of gravity.

The Six Realms

Buddhism holds that there are six different realms into which one can be reborn. *First*, there is the human realm which we all currently inhabit.

Second, there is the realm of the animals, who are ignorant and incapable of understanding the *Dharma*.

Third, there is the realm of the gods: we previously saw that Buddhism does not deny that there are gods, but claims that gods, like humans and animals, are involved in the cycle of samsara. Divine pleasures will not last for ever, and once the lifespan of a god or goddess is ended, he or she will be reborn in one of the other five realms.

Fourth, there is the realm of the *asuras*, or 'anti-gods' (sometimes called 'titans'). These beings covet the realm of the gods and engage in combat to gain access to a tree of life. Although they are coveting something desirable, their aims are misguided, since the *asuras* should be seeking enlightenment, not the pleasures of the gods' realm.

Fifth, there is the realm of the *pretas*, or hungry ghosts. These wraith-like beings are often portrayed with swollen bellies and pin-sized mouths which prevent them from satisfying their hunger. When any food or drink touches their lips it is transformed into something totally revolting and inedible. Wraiths or ghosts have always been somewhat of a puzzle to humankind: do they really exist?; why are they not properly dead?; how can they be 'laid' to rest or exorcised? In Buddhist thought, ghosts are as real as any other being who is caught up in the wheel of samsara; they are ghosts because this is the appropriate consequence of some of their past *karma*, and they will cease to be ghosts when these elements of their *karma* are burned out and they are enabled to pass on to a subsequent existence in another of the six realms.

Sixth, and finally, there are the hells. In Buddhism it is often stated that there is not merely one hell, but many. Often their very names are enough to indicate what the unfortunate offender might expect: 'Molten Brass', 'Flowing Fire', 'Ploughing Tongues', 'Head Chopping', 'Burning Feet', 'Flying Knives', 'Eye Pecking', and 'Much Hatred'. Buddhist writings sometimes give gruesome descriptions of these states. Here is one:

> There is a hell in which the offender's tongue is stretched out and ploughed through by cattle; there is a hell in which the offender's heart is pulled out and eaten by *yaksas* [demons]; there is a hell in which the offender's body is fried in cauldrons of seething broth; there is a hell in which

the offender is made to embrace a red-hot bronze pillar; there is a hell in which the offender is followed everywhere by fire; there is a hell in which there is cold and ice; there is a hell in which there is limitless dung and urine; there is a hell in which there are flying maces; there is a hell in which there are many fiery spears; there is a hell in which one is constantly beaten on the chest and back; there is a hell in which one's hands and feet are burned; there is a hell in which the offender is wrapped and bound by iron serpents; there is a hell in which there are running iron dogs; and there is a hell in which the offender is yoked between iron donkeys.[2]

If one wonders how one can survive these hells for any length of time, the answer is that one is constantly revived in order to experience continued torment. Flying knives may kill, but one can die and be reborn hundreds of times within a single moment. Different Buddhists will understand the hells in different ways: some take these descriptions literally; others view them as symbolic of states of torment which must be undergone in human lives as a result of misdeeds. Thus a hell-being might be viewed as a person in acute mental torment, or a god as someone who experiences every comfort in life: someone might move from one realm to another within the same earthly existence. There is one thing on which Buddhists would agree, however: the hells are not the handiwork of some malevolent being. They are the products of ourselves, created by our own evil *karma*.

Nirvana

To escape from these six realms is to reach nirvana, the ultimate goal of the Buddhist. Nirvana is difficult, indeed impossible to define; it is much easier to say what nirvana is *not* than it is to state what nirvana *is*. Although Buddhists sometimes speak of 'entering' nirvana, unlike the Christian concept of the kingdom of heaven, nirvana is not a place in a spiritual world where enlightened people go after death. Yet nirvana is not oblivion. What we can say is that it is the only state which is truly worth attaining and which is not subject to the unsatisfactoriness of our present physical world. Nirvana is something which cannot be understood fully until it is experienced. There is a Buddhist fable which illustrates this point, and which is worth quoting.

Once upon a time there lived a fish and a turtle who were friends. The fish, having lived all his life in the water knew nothing whatever about anything else. One day, as the fish was swimming in the water, he met his friend, the turtle, who had just returned from an excursion on land. On being told this, the fish said, 'On dry land! What do you mean by "dry land"? I have never seen such a thing — "dry land" is nothing!'

'Well,' said the turtle, 'you are at liberty to think so, but that is where I have been all the same.'

'O, come,' said the fish, 'try to talk sense. Just tell me, what is this "land" of yours like? Is it all wet?'

'No, it is not wet,' said the turtle.

'Is it nicely fresh and cool?' asked the fish.

'No, it is not fresh and cool,' replied the turtle.

'Is it clear, so that light can come through it?'

'No, it is not clear. Light cannot come through it.'

'Is it soft and yielding, so that I can move my fins about in it and push my nose through it?'

'No, it is not soft and yielding. You cannot swim in it.'

'Does it move or flow in streams? Does it ever rise up into waves with white foam on them?' asked the fish, becoming rather impatient at the string of No's.

'No, replied the turtle, it never rises up into waves.'

'The fish then asked, 'If the land is not a single one of these things, what else is it but nothing?'

'Well,' said the turtle, 'if you are determined to think that "dry land" is nothing, I cannot help you. But anyone who knows what is water and what is land would say you were a silly fish for you think that anything you have never known is nothing just because *you* have never known it.'[3]

The Two Levels of Truth

Far from meaning extinction, it is only nirvana which is real, according to the Buddhist. Everything else is subject to delusion. Not only the self is illusory, but the entire physical world is riddled with delusion.

It may be puzzling to be told that we do not see the world as it really is. Does this mean that we are constantly hallucinating? Has the Buddhist no means of distinguishing between the illusory mirage and the real oasis in the desert? Or does this mean that if I were a Buddhist I would be lying if I told you that I was really and truly sitting in a real room, writing a real book?

One Buddhist thinker who lived in the second century CE was particularly influential in trying to explain this. His name was Nagarjuna, and most Buddhist thinkers today accept his doctrine of the 'two levels of truth'.

His teaching can be explained as follows. There is 'conventional truth' and there is 'ultimate truth'. Conventional truth is what we accept most of the time, barring human error. It is conventionally true that I am sitting at a table, writing this book, since anyone else who happened to watch me would agree. It would be 'conventionally false' to believe that I was Ronald Reagan and used to star in Hollywood films — most people would regard me as insane if I claimed that this were true.

But what we conventionally accept as a true statement is not an 'ultimate truth', for the author George Chryssides is no permanent enduring being, and this book is not a permanently enduring book. But it is an 'ultimate truth' that there are three Marks of Existence — impermanence, the absence of a permanent self, and unsatisfactoriness — and someone who has reached nirvana recognises this. However, if asked 'How many people are in this room?' an enlightened person would not say 'none', for even the very few who are enlightened still have to live out the remainder of their lives in the world of our conventions.

A further example might help to explain this, but it must be remembered that it is only a rough analogy. Tables and chairs look solid, but a physicist will tell us that they are really large bundles of atomic particles, swirling round in constant motion. 'Conventionally' the table looks solid, but in reality most of it is empty space. Yet what physicist has ever refused to sit in a chair because it is not solid or not stationary? Although the physicist may have discovered the real nature of chairs, he or she will still act in the conventional way when it comes to sitting down.

Something like this is true of enlightenment. When nirvana is reached, tables and chairs do not seem to disappear into oblivion. In fact, the everyday world must exist if it is constantly changing. The enlightened one does not see something different from the unenlightened, but 'something more' in the world of samsara in which enlightened and unenlightened alike both live.

Notes to Chapter 3

1   Buddhists regard the mind as a sense in addition to the five which are acknowledged in the West.
2   Hsuan Hua, *Sutra of the Past Vows of Earth Store Bodhisattva* (Buddhist Text Translation Society, The Institute for Advanced Studies of World Religions, 1974) pp 140–141
3   H Saddhatissa, *What is Nibbana?* (British Mahabodhi Society, London, 1984) pp 9–11

4

Monks and Lay Followers

The Sangha is formed

Becoming a member of the Sangha (the community of monks) was initially a matter of responding to the Buddha's simple invitation to join, but as time went on various conditions were imposed. Anyone who wanted to commit his life to the Sangha had to vow that he was a free man, that he had no debts, that he was not in royal service, that he was over 20 years old and that he had his parents' consent. This was to ensure that the members of Sangha had not joined to escape a master, a creditor or military service. Joining became a ceremony in which the novice repeated three times the triple formula:

> I take the Buddha as my refuge.
> I take the Dharma as my refuge.
> I take the Sangha as my refuge.

We have seen how the first orders of monks known as the Sangha were formed. The Buddha ordained nuns as well as monks, but the female orders have died out in the Theravada tradition. In some Theravada orders, it is possible for women to lead lives which are very similar to those of the monks, but they do not become ordained and do not take on the title '*bhikkhuni*'. In the Mahayana traditions, however, both monks and nuns are found today.

Before ordination, one's hair is shaved off as a sign that one's previous secular life is being discarded. The monk also receives a spiritual name, often one which is somehow appropriate to his personality or what he must strive to become. A name of one of the Buddha's close followers might be possible — for example, Subhuti or Sariputra — or one might receive a name which designates an office, such as '*Dharmarakshita*' (meaning, 'keeper of the teachings'). The spiritual name indicates a kind of negation of the self, as well as a break with the monk's past secular life.

A Theravadin monk is not permitted to own possessions. He has the use of three robes (an under-garment, an outer garment and a cloak): for the traditional Theravadin monk, these will be saffron in colour; in other traditions they could be maroon (as in Tibetan), or black (as in Zen). Sandals may be worn, but Theravadin monks often regard them as a luxury. (Whether they are a luxury or a necessity depends on a country's climate, so variations in the details of these practices are to be expected.) In addition to one's clothing, a limited amount of equipment is permitted: an alms bowl (with carrying strap), a belt, a razor, a needle for mending, a waist-band or belt and a strainer. The purpose of the strainer is to filter out any minute living creatures in one's water: all forms of life are to be respected.

There is no fixed pattern as to where a monk lives. Some have no fixed abode, and wander in the open air, often in forests or mountains, sleeping under trees. Others live in caves or in huts which they have made from leaves or pieces of wood. More common, however, is life in a *vihara*: the word literally means 'dwelling-place', and *viharas* are usually unpretentious, often indistinguishable from ordinary homes. If for some reason a *vihara* is unusually large or important, it can be called a monastery. Some fairly large properties are owned by Buddhist communities, often having been put at the disposal of the Sangha by wealthy benefactors, such as royalty or successful businessmen. If the monastic community is large, there will be a division of labour, with delegated tasks such as receiving guests, maintaining the water supplies or ensuring that robes or alms bowls are in serviceable condition. In some Zen monasteries, monks may be required to do gardening, but this task would never be given to a Theravadin monk, since tilling the soil involves killing worms and small insects, and would therefore violate their monastic precepts. In smaller communities, each member of the Sangha will pursue his or her own simple life.

Theravada Buddhism tends to be loosely structured. Unlike Christianity, with its hierarchy of cardinals, bishops, moderators and the like, each Sangha is responsible to itself alone. There is no presidential figure or national assembly which demands obedience or is available for consultation in the event of problems. Within a Theravadin *vihara* one monk will be regarded as the senior monk: this is determined neither by age nor by ballot, but by the length of time one has been ordained. The structure of Tibetan and Japanese Buddhism is somewhat different: in the Tibetan tradition, special veneration is given to incarnate lamas and of course to the Dalai Lama. In Japanese orders a hierarchy of priests and sometimes a high priest is to be found.

In a Theravadin monastery or *vihara*, the monastic day starts very early, often at four o'clock in the morning. It begins with chanting, and then the monks will go into the nearest village to do their alms round, which provides them with breakfast. Members of the laity will bring them their mid-day meal, and local residents often arrange a rota system amongst themselves to do this. The monk does not ask for food, in contrast to the beggar who does: it is therefore incorrect to describe his bowl as a 'begging bowl', as westerners often do. The monk will wait patiently for a short time outside each house: if no food is brought out, he will move on. When he has received sufficient food, he will return to his dwelling place. (In some communities where the day begins later, the alms round provides the mid-day meal.)

It is a mistake to think that Buddhists are always vegetarian. Most western Buddhists are, but a monk is not supposed to refuse any food he is given, with few exceptions. If he suspects that an animal has been specially killed for him, this would be unacceptable. Also, food must be prepared and ready to eat. Raw ingredients will not do, for two reasons: *first*, members of the traditional Sangha do not cook, and, *second*, the willingness to accept cooked food underlines the

A Buddhist monk on an alms round
Photograph: Philip Emmett

Buddhist's rejection of the Indian caste system. In India, in the Buddha's time, it was normal for lay people only to accept prepared food from members of equal caste; by accepting food from everyone, regardless of their status, the Buddhist monk demonstrates that the Sangha is outside the Hindu caste system. Monks are permitted to accept invitations to eat at people's homes, as did the Buddha and his early followers when invited back to his father's palace.

Food must be consumed by noon, after which the monk does not eat. Although this is foreign to our way of life, Buddhist monks to whom I have spoken insist that their eating habits are preferable to ours, since we tend to eat our largest meal late in the day, at a time when no subsequent physical exercise is taken.

The remainder of the day is relatively unstructured. A monk may teach younger disciples, or he may read in order to further his study, or he may meditate in silence. He may also have personal tasks requiring attention. It is tempting to think in our western armchairs that all Buddhist monks are developing themselves spiritually in this calm of meditative existence. But, just as there are good and bad clergy in Christianity, there are good and bad monks, and it would not be unknown for an occasional monk to spend the afternoon half asleep instead of being in the concentrated state which meditation requires!

The Precepts

The traditional Theravadin monk undertakes to observe a number of precepts. Altogether there are 227 of these; but there are normally ten main precepts. There is slight variation in content, but the list generally runs as follows:

1   To avoid the taking of life.
2   To avoid taking what is not given.
3   To avoid unchastity.
4   To avoid incorrect speech.
5   To avoid intoxicating liquor and drugs, which lead to carelessness.

6　To avoid eating at improper times.

7　To avoid dancing, singing, and seeing public entertainments.

8　To avoid wearing garlands and using scents, ornaments and finery.

9　To avoid using a high or luxurious sleeping place.

10　To avoid handling gold or silver (*ie*, money).

Theravadin monks do not marry, but married monks (sometimes called priests) are not uncommon in Mahayana Buddhism. Members of the Theravadin Sangha have strict rules about relationships with women. A monk may not be alone with a woman or touch her. Sexual misconduct is a particularly serious offence, for which a monk can be suspended from the Order. If he is discovered to have had a sexual relationship with a woman, the penalty is expulsion.

The Laity

Most people's attention has focussed on the Buddhist monk, perhaps because he is a seemingly strange figure whose lifestyle differs so markedly from ours. However, we must not stereotype the Buddhist as the saffron-robed monk who meditates constantly in order to gain enlightenment. The majority of Buddhists are lay people, and indeed the Sangha could not exist if there were not a laity to support it.

Just as one cannot be born a monk, one cannot be born a Buddhist lay person either. A lay Buddhist is one who has taken the three-fold Refuge:

> I take the Buddha as my refuge.
> I take the Dharma as my refuge.
> I take the Sangha as my refuge.

In order to become a Buddhist, one would normally recite the Triple Refuge in the presence of a monk. Lay persons may take on precepts, but, unlike the Sangha, this is done gradually, when the follower is ready. For example, one may be a convert to Buddhism, but not yet ready to give up alcohol. In the meantime, the convert will probably decide not to drink to excess: perhaps one day he or she will give it up completely. And if this Buddhist attends a ceremony in which precepts are recited, he or she will remain silent when the precept proscribing alcohol is said.

At first appearance it seems that the monk is being parasitic on the laity. It is only because the laity grow crops and earn money that the monk is enabled to pursue the contemplative life without distractions. Since monks are not community workers, the laity appears to gain nothing directly in return. If a lay Buddhist wants to achieve a practical goal, like securing a good harvest, or passing an examination, in the Theravadin tradition at least, one would not normally pray to the Buddha or expect the Sangha to do so. Monks are not like Hindu or Christian priests, who act as mediators between gods and human beings, and they would certainly not use spiritual means to secure material benefits for the populace.

Rites of Passage and Death

Even rites of passage, such as birth and marriage need not involve the Sangha: lay Buddhists would be much more inclined to mark such events by ceremonies connected with other religions which co-exist alongside Buddhism. Some Buddhists will ask a monk to bless their marriage or read scriptures before the wedding takes place. New parents may provide food for the monks to mark the birth of their child, since giving alms to the Sangha brings merit to the donor, helping to ensure a good rebirth. But these are not prescribed ceremonies or acts.

Death, however, is different. Monks usually are asked to officiate at funerals and this provides an opportunity for monks and lay people alike to be reminded that everything is transient. Theravadin monks take the opportunity provided by a funeral to preach on life's impermanence and death's inevitability. Death is the event which separates one rebirth from the next, and the death of a friend or relative, as well as an occasion for grief, is a salutary reminder that everyone present is also subject to death, and must gain sufficient merit to secure a good rebirth.

Of all the varieties of Buddhism, the Tibetan tradition lays the greatest emphasis on death. When someone's life has ended it is common for *The Tibetan Book of the Dead* to be recited over the corpse. This book gives instructions for the guidance of spirits after death. (Tibetan Buddhism commonly believes that one has a spirit body, or 'astral body', which is connected to the physical body during life, but becomes severed from it at death. Those who have clairvoyant powers are said to be able to see the astral body in the form of an aura around a living person, and can tell when someone has died by apprehending its departure.)

It is held that for 49 days after death, the spirit hovers around the body. It sees many visions of lights and buddha-figures attempting to guide it either towards the six realms in which rebirth occurs, or else towards nirvana. *The Tibetan Book of the Dead* gives instructions to the spirit about how to interpret these after-death experiences and how to attain enlightenment in this after-death state. Because the spirit cannot normally be seen or heard, it does not necessarily follow that the spirit cannot see or hear what is happening in the physical world it has just left — hence there is believed to be tremendous value in offering to the spirit the guidance which this book has to offer.

Whether or not *The Tibetan Book of the Dead* is used, Buddhists agree that it is important to approach death with as clear and unclouded a mind as possible. For this reason, a Buddhist will avoid receiving drugs such as morphine which reduce the level of consciousness or speed up the dying process. Having 'perfect view' and 'perfect mindfulness' involves experiencing death in as fully conscious a state as possible.

After the body has been disposed of in the customary manner, a symbolic effigy of the deceased is installed in the house, and readings, prayers and food offerings are given. Ideally, one should not wait until one has died to learn what *The Book of the Dead* has to teach: appropriate study during one's lifetime will enable the Buddhist to know in advance what to expect on meeting death. However, only a small proportion of Tibetans would actually possess copies of the book, or indeed be able to read its contents.

In other Buddhist traditions, the laity will give donations to the Sangha in exchange for the monks reciting portions of scripture, thus bestowing merit on the deceased, so that he or she might be reborn well. Chanting is performed at various times in the 49 day period after a death, and also on the monthly or annual anniversaries of the death.

The Sangha's Contribution

Apart from times of bereavement, there is little which the monks directly *do* for the laity. However, it is not expected that the Sangha should act as community workers, and westerners have often failed to understand lay people's expectations of the Sangha by inadvertently comparing the little Buddhist monasteries scattered around the East with the small village churches one finds in a country like Britain. In 1892, the Anglican Bishop of Colombo visited a Sinhalese monastery, and during his visit asked a villager whether the monks did any good in the village. The villager's response was, 'No, why should they?'!

This may seem surprising. However, every religion is faced with the dilemma of whether to apply small bandages to heal specific isolated sores in society, or whether to attempt major surgery to get to the root of humankind's fundamental problems. The monks do the latter by giving teachings, which, if put into practice by everyone, would get rid of the root causes of unsatisfactoriness. If everyone were to follow the precepts and the Eightfold Path, ignorance and selfish desire — which lie at the root of all ills — would disappear.

In Theravadin countries, it is usually necessary to become a monk in order to be enlightened, dispelling the three 'fires' of ignorance, greed and hatred. Many of the laity support the Sangha, hoping that one day too, perhaps in a future rebirth, they would be able to take on the robe and lead the meditative life, relying on others to support them.

There is a possible compromise for lay men. Becoming a member of the Sangha need not be a permanent commitment, and it is not uncommon for laymen to take the robe and live in a monastic community for short periods of time, perhaps even just for a fortnight. Such action is held to bring merit to the one who does it, and at some future date the possibility of rejoining the order may lie open. Monks and lay people are therefore not totally separate.

Devotions

Members of the Sangha will generally take responsibility for conducting devotions (*puja*). As ever, there are variations in accordance with local traditions; however, a typical Theravadin *puja* might take the following form. (This is the order followed by the London Buddhist Vihara.)

At the beginning, homage is paid by all participants to the Buddha, Dharma and Sangha, the 'Three Refuges'. The congregation recites the Five Precepts (the first five of the Ten Precepts mentioned earlier). Flowers, lights (candles) and incense are then offered by being passed round the congregation. Verses are recited in praise of the Three Refuges, after which the senior monk delivers a short sermon. A short piece of scripture is then recited. (The *Karaniya Metta Sutta* — 'Discourse on Loving Kindness' — would be suitable.) The congregation then spends a short time in meditation, and the *puja* ends with blessings (*mangalas*) being said.

Festivals

It might be expected that the Sangha has a large role in Buddhist festivals. This is not the case. Monks will play some part in festivals, but, since the monks' primary concern is nirvana, they will involve themselves as little as possible in the preparations and activities. Although the populace may use such occasions as an excuse for festivity, and the monks

Shrine room, London Buddhist Vihara
Photograph: George Chryssides

may co-operate by making public processions, festivals are not primarily celebrations: they are for devotion and increasing spiritual merit. This is done by observing the precepts more strictly than usual during a festival day. In Burma and Tibet, for example, special kindness is shown to animals, and the laity might rescue animals from slaughter-houses or take fish out of dried-up river beds and place them in freshwater ponds.

One festival which is marked by all Buddhists is the festival of *Wesak* (sometimes called 'Buddha Day'), commemorating the birth of the Buddha. This falls on the last full moon in May. In the Theravada tradition it marks the birth, enlightenment and death of the Buddha simultaneously. A Buddhist once remarked to me, 'It's like celebrating Christmas, Easter and Whitsun all at once!' But even at Wesak there is little festivity — only a short procession, some chanting, scripture reading and meditation.

During the three month monsoon period (roughly July to October), Theravadin monks go into retreat. This is partly to ensure their own shelter, and partly because farmers formerly complained that monks were trampling their crops into the mud in their wanderings! When the rains begin, villagers give food, medicines and clothes to the monks, who deliver teachings in return. Some of the laity will retreat with the monks for all or part of the monsoon season. Young boys of eight or over, who are permitted to be ordained as novices (not fully fledged monks), will ask to be admitted to a monastery at this time. This is sometimes accompanied by a piece of pageantry, in which boys are decked with fine clothes and process on animals through their village to the monastery, where their fine clothes are removed, their heads shaven and they take on the robe. They will stay in the monastery with the monks for at least a night, and in many cases for a longer period. Girls too can take part in the pageant in similar vein, but they do not join the Sangha.

After the rainy season has ended, the *Kathina* festival takes place: the monks process, and villagers go to the monasteries to present raw cotton cloth, which the monks then dye saffron (or red, as appropriate) to make new robes. Villagers celebrate this festival for several days with dancing, singing and plays. The monks, of course, do not attend these, as this would be a violation of the monastic precepts.

Inside the monastery, it is common for *Uposatha* ('Observance Day') to be celebrated twice monthly. As with other 'festivals', fasting and especially strict observance of the precepts is the order of the day. At every second celebration of Observance Day, monks confess any misdeeds they have committed. They assemble in the shrine room on low seats, whereupon the senior monk begins by chanting, and then solicits confessions. If there is silence, he says: 'Pure of these misdeeds are the Venerable Ones. That is why they have kept silent. Thus have I heard it.' If any monk is guilty of misconduct and remains silent, this is tantamount to speaking falsely, and is a serious breach of the monastic precepts.

To sum up, the monk follows the Buddhist path in one way, the laity in another. The Sangha does not offer very much by way of direct physical help, but provides teachings which, if practised, would provide humankind with a means of resolving the unsatisfactoriness of human life.

5

Buddhist Meditation

Buddhism is associated primarily with meditation, and the serene figure of Gautama the Buddha gaining enlightenment under the sacred pipal tree provides an example for Buddhists to follow. Meditation takes various forms, depending on the tradition, or the purpose. Some meditations are silent, others are noisy, others have an elaborate liturgy interspersed with periods of silence; some are guided by a meditation leader, while in others the participants sit and meditate in whatever style they have learned. In most types of meditation, meditators sit on the floor facing a buddha-image. As the eyes close, the image of the Buddha is the last thing one sees. Incense is burned in front of the Buddha, and flowers and offerings of fruit are often present. Sometimes candles are lit.

A normal 'sitting' can be anything from 20 to 45 minutes, or even longer. The meditator is usually instructed to sit on a meditation cushion in a cross-legged position, with back upright and shoulders straight, and with the head forward. Slouching is forbidden, but muscles should not be tensed into position. Hands are placed on one's lap: some Buddhists will allow the thumb and index finger of each hand to touch, forming a circle (the 'symbol of knowledge pose'); other meditation teachers recommend resting hands on top of each other, palms upwards. Clasping the hands is discouraged, as clasping creates a degree of muscle tension.

Unwanted thoughts will probably arise, which take the mind away from the meditation. Meditators are recommended simply to notice that these thoughts arise and to realise that this is quite normal. They should not become upset that this is happening, but should gently bring the mind back to the meditation once more, having noted the thought which caused the distraction. By merely noting the thoughts that arise and letting them pass, the meditator develops non-attachment to them, and learns to focus the mind on whatever is the current object of attention.

Among the many varieties of Buddhist meditation, it is useful to select a number for special description. It is worth pointing out that what follows is intended merely as information about Buddhism, and not as an instruction manual for would-be meditators. A Buddhist will normally meditate only under the guidance of a suitably qualified teacher who will ensure that the student adopts an appropriate practice and receives suitable guidance about his or her progress.

1   Mindfulness of Breathing

Normally when we breathe we are unaware of what we are doing. Breathing is a 'semi-voluntary' activity: that is to say, left to their own devices, the lungs will normally get on efficiently with their job. However, once we focus our attention on our breathing, we find that we can alter it by shortening, lengthening or holding breaths. In 'Mindfulness of Breathing', the meditator focusses attention on the tip of the nose, and attempts to become aware of the breath without altering it: it is not like a yoga breathing exercise. This may sound easy, but most people will find it hard to allow even a few breaths to pass without losing track of them. A frequent instruction is to focus on the point of entry and exit of the breath in the body — a very delicate sensation which can continually elude all but the most proficient meditator.

By gaining awareness of something of which one is not normally aware, the Buddhist is helped to acquire 'perfect mindfulness' — the seventh step of the Buddhist Eightfold Path.

2   'Metta Bhavana'

Buddhist meditation is not always 'inward-looking'. In the meditation called 'Metta Bhavana' one is trying to cultivate good feelings towards other people. *Bhavana* means 'cultivation' and *metta* means 'loving-kindness'.

The meditation is in five stages. In the course of the meditation one focusses one's mind successively on:

1 oneself;
2 a close friend;
3 someone to whom one is indifferent;
4 someone to whom one feels hostile;
5 all four at once, in such a way as to cultivate an evenness of affection to each.

The important thing in this meditation is to develop *feelings* of affection towards the people one has selected, not to intellectualise by compiling a kind of 'shopping-list' of their good points. The meditator should envisage situations in which the various people had a sense of well-being, or some situation in which he or she has experienced good relationships with the friend, 'neutral person' or enemy. It is important to concentrate on the positive, good situations, and not the bad. The meditator is instructed to think the thought, 'May that person be happy; may he (or she) be well'.

In order to develop an evenness of affection in the final stage, one might think of a situation where these four people are all together. Perhaps one can imagine having a present and being unable to decide to whom one should give it. According to one Buddhist source, I should imagine a scene where robbers enter my house, demanding that I give up one person to be killed, and I genuinely cannot decide who to surrender to them. Normally we would consider that if there is any doubt in such situations, I should at least ensure that I give other people preferential treatment. This is discouraged by the meditation, since oneself is neither more nor less worthy of affection than another. Indeed, in order to be able to show kindness or compassion successfully, I have to become the right sort of person first.

The results of *Metta Bhavana* are often unexpected: one might suppose that the meditator would find it most difficult to love the enemy; however, many practitioners find that the real problem lies with the 'neutral person', the one to whom they are indifferent and have no genuine feelings one way or the other.

3 *Walking, Standing and Lying*

Not all meditation is done sitting on a cushion. The person who is 'aware' is not just aware of breathing, but of everything else that is occurring in his or her body. Few of us are aware of how we perform a simple task like walking. We normally find it confusing to stop and ask ourselves which foot we start with, for when it comes to activities in which we are well practised, our body functions on 'automatic pilot', virtually bypassing the mind. If we are to become 'aware', therefore, we must focus on every single movement that the body makes.

Meditation is intended to do this. There are four main postures which are adopted, at various times — sitting, walking, standing and lying down. In walking, the meditator picks a straight walking path, the extremities of which are between 15 and 25 paces apart. Hands are clasped, either in front or behind, and then the walk commences — walking, stopping, turning, being aware of every movement of the foot, as it lifts, advances and touches the ground. Walking meditation is often done extremely slowly, but some monks recommend that a normal walking pace is adopted, since we should be able to be mindful in the daily walking we have to do.

The idea of walking or standing with no particular aim may seem strange, but it enables the meditator to cut out thoughts which normally intrude when we stand or walk for a particular purpose. If I am walking to meet a friend, I may be thinking, 'Am I late?' or 'Is this the right evening?'; if I am standing, waiting for a bus, I may begin to feel impatient, wondering, 'When will the bus come?'. 'Just walking' or 'just standing' ensures that intrusive thoughts like these are not present and that the meditator can concentrate on what the body is doing.

4 *The Contemplation of the Body*

The 'Contemplation of the Body' includes a practice which is designed to create awareness of our conventional self and to demonstrate the unsatisfactoriness of human existence. As a prelude to this meditation, some orders of monks recite the following:

> In this body are: hair of the head, hair of the body, nails, teeth, skin, flesh, sinews, bones, bone-marrow, kidneys, heart, liver, membranes, spleen, lungs, bowels, entrails, undigested food, excrement, bile, phlegm, pus, blood, sweat, fat, tears, grease, spittle, mucus, oil of the joints, urine and brain.

The words are not meant to be pleasant. Although most monastic communities who have used this meditation have chanted it in the original Pali, one Buddhist group in Great Britain now makes a point of reciting it in English, so that its impact is not lost. Once the chanting is done, meditators take their attention through their bodies, starting at the top of the head, working their way down to the feet. They need not go through every item on the list. When a Theravadin monk is first ordained, he is often instructed to contemplate the first five items on the list, since hair (of the head and body), nails, teeth and skin have possibly been objects of vanity in his former secular life.

Meditators are expected to become aware of how unsatisfactory the body is. To realise that the body is impure is to ensure that they do not remain attached to this unsatisfactory physical world. Yet at the same time they should not focus only on what is unpleasant, for someone who is enlightened sees things as they really are. Human hair or skin can indeed sometimes be beautiful, and this should be recognised. However, because the world is impermanent and constantly changing, in another context these bodily parts can be unpleasant — for example, if I am about to take a bath and discover that the previous user (who is otherwise attractive) has left strands of hair and pieces of dead skin which have formed into scum!

The important point is to adopt 'perfect view' with regard to the body, neither rejecting it completely nor believing it to be wholly satisfactory. The Buddha himself, before he became enlightened, adopted these two extremes with regard to his body. In the royal palace he pampered his body with luxury; in the forest he made his body suffer with hunger and austerity, as if it were evil. Adopting the Middle Way involves understanding the body and creating a tranquil mind which can accept whatever happens to the body, whether it is pleasant or painful.

5   'Recollection of Death'

A Buddhist should not have 'perfect mindfulness' only about life. It is important to adopt the correct attitude towards death. Meditation can aid this too. It is sometimes said that Buddhism is a 'religion of death'. The Buddha's renunciation of the world was influenced by seeing the funeral procession. The Buddha taught that everything is constantly dying because it is impermanent; Buddhism teaches that death is not something final but a bridge between one existence and the next. It is understandable, then, that death should be a theme in meditation.

One straight-forward meditation on death is outlined as follows:

> In 'the recollection of death', the word 'death' refers to the cutting off of the life-force which lasts for the length of one existence. Whoso wants to develop it, should in seclusion and solitude wisely set up attention with the words: 'Death will take place, the life-force will be cut off,' or (simply), 'Death, death'.[1]

In some forms of 'the recollection of death', one is encouraged to look at death from various points of view, for example, as a murderer, as a sudden unexpected happening, by considering others who have died, and so on. Another practice consists of envisaging a corpse in various stages of decomposition, and in certain monasteries monks are even instructed to go to a cremation ground at night and perform 'the recollection of death' there.

To westerners, all this may seem gruesome and macabre, for death is really a taboo subject in the West. (The taboo subjects are not sex, politics and religion, as is sometimes said.) For the Buddhist, by contrast, it is important to see death — as well as everything else — as it really is. It is common to see the frequent use of skulls in Buddhist art and depicted in shrine-rooms, particularly in the Tibetan tradition. I once visited a Tibetan shrine in which lifesize models of skeletons were hanging. This is a constant reminder that everything is impermanent (*anicca*), including the physical life that we are living. We should not start to think of death only when a doctor tells us that we have an incurable illness. In a sense, we are all terminally ill, because we are suffering from the disease of attachment to life, the cure for which can be found in the Buddhist path.

6 Visualisation

The meditations described so far are practised within the Theravada tradition. Visualisation is used particularly in the *Vajrayana* (see Chapter Seven). This consists of taking a pictorial image of a buddha or a bodhisattva (called one's *yidam*), and gazing at it. After some time, the meditator closes his or her eyes and attempts to reconstruct mentally the image which has been seen in all its detail.

This sounds easy enough until one actually tries it. Readers who have played party games which require participants to remember objects on a tray, or points of detail in a relatively simple picture, will realise how unreliable the memory can be. In the case of images of buddhas and bodhisattvas, the detail involved is very complex indeed and sustained efforts at meditation are required before the *yidam* is absorbed. Even after gazing for half an hour, it is possible to wonder, once the eyes are closed, whether (say) Avalokiteshvara is holding his rosary on the right hand or the left, or whether the left leg crosses the right or vice versa.

Why meditate?

Having been given this account of Buddhist meditation, an external observer may fail to see the purpose of these meditative practices. Why should some Buddhists devote their lives to meditation when instead they could be designing sophisticated computer equipment or engaging in medical

Avalokiteshvara when reproducing
© *Wisdom Publications. Reproduced by permission.*

research, which would seem to benefit humanity in more obvious ways? Why endeavour to walk slowly when you can reach your destination much more quickly by walking fast, or by using our technological achievements such as cars, aircraft or satellites? And how can reconstructing a picture in the mind be anything more than a remarkable party trick?

It is important to answer these banal questions, or else we miss the point of Buddhist practice. The Buddhist who practises walking meditation need not deny that it is sometimes necessary for us to be in a hurry, and to rely on modern technology for fast transport. One obvious answer is that computers, medicines, cars and aeroplanes all enhance humankind's physical needs, but do little to further its spiritual ones. Although scientific achievements show what the human mind can achieve, they do not make us aware of what the mind is, and its thoughts, emotions and volitions which cause unsatisfactoriness. The healthy and the wealthy are not free from unsatisfactoriness, and neither modern technology nor medicine can eliminate *dukkha*. Asking meditators to concentrate on something apparently trivial, such as walking or standing, helps them to let go of prejudices about what is important and what is not. It is important to become aware of things as they really are, and as the meditator becomes more able to expand insight to more and more aspects of life, 'perfect view' is being achieved.

Visualisation likewise is to enable the meditator to progress along the spiritual path. It is, *first*, an act of devotion to the buddha or bodhisattva who is visualised, and who provides the spiritual ideal to be attained. *Second*, and equally important, visualisation enables the meditator to internalise the buddha- or bodhisattva-nature. If the meditator lacks wisdom (and we all lack wisdom until we become enlightened), then visualising Manjushri — the Bodhisattva of Wisdom — helps to bestow that virtue. If we need to increase our compassion (and we all lack complete compassion as long as there are unenlightened living beings around), our compassion increases as we create Avalokiteshvara inside ourselves. Of course, the meditator does not decide by himself or herself what virtues are needed, or which *yidam* should be used: this is something for the teacher to prescribe.

7   *Vipassana Meditation*

Meditation also has a close relationship with Buddhist teachings. It is used not only to calm the mind but to enable the meditator to experience the truth of Buddhist doctrines. When meditation is done for this purpose it is called *Vipassana* or 'insight' meditation.

We have seen that the three Marks of Existence are impermanence, the absence of self or soul, and unsatisfactoriness. Turning the mind through meditation upon the breath or upon the body can enable the meditator to recognise how impermanent, insubstantial and unsatisfactory everything really is. To recognise the delicacy of the breath which keeps someone alive enables the Buddhist to experience how impermanent human life is; the meditator who contemplates the body and its experiences does not find any enduring soul inside, but discovers instead how unsatisfactory the human body is.

8   *Following the thought*

There is a particular technique which some Buddhist teachers of meditation use for dealing with wandering thoughts. This consists of a meditation called 'Following the Thought'. The name encapsulates the practice: one is asked to do nothing at all, but simply to note the thoughts which arise in one's mind, and to watch them come and go like passing clouds in the sky. When a thought occurs which would normally be an unwelcome distraction in the other forms of meditation we have mentioned, the meditator holds on to that thought and looks at it with attention. Inevitably some other thought will intrude to distract the meditator away from the first one; this too is noted and held until a further thought ousts it.

All in all, the various meditative practices reveal how uncontrolled the mind is and how imperfect our 'mindfulness' really is. When one comes to realise the normal state of one's mind, bringing it under control is a formidable task. As the Buddha once said:

Though one may conquer a thousand times a thousand men in battle, yet he indeed is the noblest victor who conquers himself.

Self-conquest is far better than the conquest of others. Not even a god, an angel, Mara or Brahma[2] can turn into defeat the victory of such a person who is self-subdued and ever restrained in conduct.[3]

The Five Hindrances

Anyone who has practised meditation will realise that, although instructions for meditation can often seem simple, they are notoriously difficult to carry out successfully. For example, beginners at 'Mindfulness of Breathing' are sometimes instructed to count each breath up to ten and then begin at one again. The majority of meditators have to admit that even counting ten breaths is a very difficult task. They will quickly lose track of the count or find unwanted thoughts crowding in. The Buddha himself knew of such distractions: while he was meditating under the pipal tree at Bodh Gaya, it is said that Mara, the tempter of the Buddha, made various attempts to take Gautama's mind away from meditation. On one occasion, Mara enlisted the support of some young women who danced naked in front of him to provide a distraction from his spiritual quest.

Buddhism has formulated a list of five principal hindrances to meditation. These are:

1   desire;
2   ill-will;
3   sloth and torpor;
4   excitement and worry;
5   doubt.

These are fairly self-explanatory. The meditator who is still clinging to material desires is still uncommitted to the spiritual benefits which meditation brings. Someone who feels ill-will is not in a position to combine compassion with wisdom, the two Buddhist ideals. One who is sluggish or sleepy cannot have 'perfect mindfulness', and a mind which is working overtime because of eager anticipation or apprehension cannot experience the inner peace which meditation brings.

Finally, there are many meditators who doubt or waver: particularly in the early stages, it is easy to doubt the value of meditative experiences and to question whether they are really bringing any true benefits; alternatively, an inexperienced meditator can feel that the form of meditation he or she has adopted is unproductive, and switch repeatedly from one practice to another. Any proficient meditator will affirm, however, that the benefits of meditation are not experienced instantly, and no accredited teacher of meditation will allow a novice to make rapid changes between different methods: to do so would be like a patient changing medicines after only a day or two, on the grounds that a cure had not been effected. For physical and spiritual disorders alike, cures take time, and it is important to apply the remedy faithfully and consistently.

Notes to Chapter 5

1   E Conze, *Buddhist Meditation* (Unwin Hyman Ltd, London, 1972) p 86
2   Brahma is an important Hindu god.
3   *The Dhammapada*, vv 103–105

6

What is Zen?

The 'Flower Sermon'

Like many of the so-called new religions, Zen Buddhism proved very fashionable as it swept across the United States in the 1960s, finding a strong foothold in California, the breeding ground of many varieties of religious practice. Zen is not a new form of Buddhism, but quite an ancient variety which emerged as Indian Buddhism came to China and blended with the ideas of Taoism, an ancient Chinese religion.

Although the beginnings of Zen are reckoned to have occurred in the sixth century CE, there is a legend which links Zen with Gautama, the Buddha himself. According to the story, the Buddha was once seated amidst other members of the Sangha, when a disciple came to him, offered him a golden flower, and asked him to preach the *Dharma*. The Buddha accepted the flower, held it up and gazed at it for some time in silence. After some time, the disciple smiled: he had intuitively grasped the spiritual idea which the Buddha was trying to transmit without the use of words. It is said that the smile of the disciple, Venerable Mahakasyapa, was handed down through 28 successive patriarchs, the last of whom was an Indian Buddhist teacher by the name of Bodhidharma.

Bodhidharma and the Chinese Emperor

Bodhidharma was a very fierce character and no picture of him ever shows him smiling, despite the story of the Flower

Sermon. It is said that Bodhidharma arrived in China in 520 CE and was invited to the capital by the emperor. The Chinese emperor regarded himself as a very keen follower of Buddhism, and said to Bodhidharma, 'I have built many temples and monasteries. I have copied the sacred books of the Buddha. I have supported the monasteries. Now, what merit have I gained?'

'None whatsoever, your majesty,' replied Bodhidharma.

'I don't understand,' rejoined the emperor. 'Explain to me the first principle of Buddhism.'

'Vast emptiness,' replied Bodhidharma.

'If everything is emptiness, then who is now standing in front of me?'

'I have absolutely no idea!' replied Bodhidharma.

These stories need a certain amount of explaining. Bodhidharma's last point is, of course, a reference to the notion that there is no self, according to Buddhist teaching. Since there is no permanent self or soul, then, strictly, there existed no Bodhidharma and no Chinese emperor. The emperor's mistake was to be concerned with personal merit rather than attaining enlightenment or, as Zen Buddhists prefer to call it, *satori*.

Both stories show the importance of going beyond the conventional trappings of religion. The emperor was taught that religious practices were insufficient for spiritual advancement. Words — our main form of communication — are insufficient to express what enlightenment means; consequently, the Buddha's 'flower sermon' was preached silently.

In the popular novel *Monkey*, the hero is a priest called Tripitaka, who makes an adventurous journey from China to India in order to collect some important scriptures. He and his companions, a monkey and a piglet, eventually find the monastery and collect the texts. They do not examine them until they are on their journey home, at which point Tripitaka discovers that they have been given nothing but blank pages. When he and his party return to complain, the resident monks give this explanation:

> As a matter of fact, it is such blank scrolls as these that are the true scriptures. But I quite see that the people of China

are too foolish and ignorant to believe this, so there is nothing for it but to give them copies with some writing on.[1]

Attitudes to Scriptures

The principles of Zen are enshrined in the following four-line summary. No one knows who wrote it — it may have been the famous Zen Master Rinzai (died 866 CE) — but most Zen Buddhists know it.

A special transmission outside the Scriptures;
No dependence upon words and letters;
Direct pointing to the heart of man;
Seeing into one's nature and being a Buddha.

There are many stories of Zen monks tearing up scriptures, or Zen Masters — such as Hakuin (1685–1768) — saying that the only proper use for scriptures was as toilet paper. It is important, however, to realise that such stories are exaggerations to jolt the mind into realising that scriptures only form part of the path to enlightenment. As a Zen teacher once remarked, the relationship between scripture and *satori* is like someone pointing a finger at the moon; only a fool would believe that the finger was the object of attention, yet at times it is useful for someone's finger to point things out to us. Similarly, scriptures are needed to shed light on the path, but they are not the destination. It is sometimes said that Zen points *above* the scriptures, whereas the Pure Land sects operate *below* them.

When scriptures are compared with toilet paper, it is worth remembering that toilet paper is not useless! Zen Buddhists do use scriptures, although the principal scriptures tend to be short ones, such as the Heart Sutra and the Diamond Sutra, thus minimising the use of words. Part of the Heart Sutra, which is short enough to engrave in its entirety on some of the rather fine calligraphers' ink-blocks, runs as follows. It is frequently chanted during meditation sittings.

So, in emptiness, no form
No feeling, thought or choice
Nor is there consciousness.

No eye, ear, nose, tongue, body, mind;
No colour, sound, smell, taste, touch
Or what the mind takes hold of
Nor even act of sensing.

No ignorance or end it
Nor all that comes of ignorance;
No withering, no death,
No end of them.

Nor is there pain or cause of pain
Or cease in pain, or noble path
To lead from pain,
Not even wisdom to attain!
Attainment too is emptiness...

All Buddhas of past and present
Buddhas of future time
Using this Prajna wisdom
Come to full and perfect vision...

No Buddhist Path?

On first appearance, the statements of the Heart Sutra seem outrageous. It is saying that there are no Noble Truths, no Eightfold Path to follow, and no ignorance to escape from. How can this be, since these are surely the fundamentals of Buddhism? Yet even in its most outrageous statements, Zen is thoroughly logical. The Truths, the Path and the human condition all belong to the physical world, which lacks an enduring unchanging quality.

Once again Zen startles the enquirer with something that seems illogical, but yet enshrines some important spiritual message which lies beyond reason. To progress on the path to *satori*, one must cleanse the mind, and, above all, meditate.

Zen meditations (*zazen* sittings, as they are called) are long and silent. The popular image of a *zazen* meditation is of novices sitting in a square formation, with a fierce Zen

Master going around with a long beating stick (a *kyosaku*) which is used copiously to discipline those who are not putting their whole effort into the meditation. It is true that the *kyosaku* is sometimes used by a meditation instructor, but it is not so much a punishment for bad meditation as a means of loosening muscles which have become stiff after sitting for an extended period in the same position. In one Zen community which I visited, the beating stick in the shrine-room was merely a symbol of the Zen tradition; the shrine-room was so small that no one could possibly have wielded it in the space available.

Clapping with one hand?

There are two main types of Zen — Soto and Rinzai. In the Rinzai school, one's mental powers are stretched to their limit — and beyond — by a device known as a *koan*. A *koan* is an enigmatic question which is set by one's spiritual master. Logically, it appears to make no sense, but to dismiss it as nonsense is not in accordance with Zen practice. The most famous *koan* is as follows: 'You have heard the sound of two hands clapping. What is the sound of one hand clapping?' Other favourite examples are, 'What did your face look like before it was born?', and 'There is a goose in a bottle. How do you get it out?'

Another *koan* goes as follows. 'A man is hanging over a precipice by his teeth, which are clenched around the branch of a tree. His hands are full and his feet cannot reach the face of the precipice. A friend leans over and asks him, "What is Zen?" What answer would you make?' One novice devised the (apparently acceptable) answer of pretending to fall from a height and exclaiming, 'Ouch, that hurt!'

There is no logical answer to most of these questions. Nevertheless the novice is required to formulate a response that comes from the buddha-nature inside oneself. The *Roshi* (Zen Master — who can be male or female) will summon the novice from the meditation session and ask questions about the prescribed *koan*, to discover what progress has been made. The *Roshi* may respond in whatever way is appropriate to help the novice to gain enlightenment: encouraging, advising, becoming angry, ridiculing, or even occasionally resorting to physical violence. There are tales of novices who have gone to all sorts of lengths to devise an acceptable sound of one hand clapping — shouting, kicking over a bucket, or turning on all the water-taps. However, it is to no avail to discover another novice whose particular answer was acceptable: what is conducive to enlightenment for someone else may not be so for me, for instance. I must discover my own buddha-nature and not someone else's.

A *Roshi* can engage the novice in a rapid exchange of cross-questioning on a *koan*. This technique is known as *mondo*, and the following is an example of a conversation based on the *koan*, 'What is the sound of the one hand?'.

> *Master*: 'If you've heard the sound of the one hand, prove it.'
> *Answer*: Without a word, the pupil thrusts one hand forward.
> *Master*: 'It's said that if one hears the sound of the one hand, one becomes a Buddha. Well then, how will you do it?'
> *Answer*: Without a word, the pupil thrusts one hand forward.
> *Master*: 'After you've become ashes, how will you hear it?'
> *Answer*: Without a word, the pupil thrusts one hand forward.
> *Master*: 'What if the one hand is cut by the Suimo sword?'
> *Answer*: 'If it can, let me see you do it.' So saying, the pupil extends his hand forward.
> *Master*: 'Why can't it cut the one hand?'
> *Answer*: 'Because the one hand pervades the universe.'
> *Master*: 'Then show me something that contains the universe.'
> *Answer*: Without a word, the pupil thrusts one hand forward.
> *Master*: 'The before-birth-one-hand, what is it like?'

Answer: Without a word, the pupil thrusts one hand forward.

Master: 'The Mount-Fuji-summit-one-hand, what is it like?'

Answer: The pupil, shading his eyes with one hand, takes the pose of looking down from the summit of Mount Fuji and says, 'What a splendid view!' naming several places to be seen from Mount Fuji — or others would name places visible from where they happen to be.[2]

The *koans* seem funny and indeed Zen Buddhists see the humour of them. In the case of the *koan*, however, it is *reason* that is the real joke; what is being ridiculed is the notion that enlightenment can be gained simply by reasoning out a series of religious truths. There is a certain logic in this. As a Zen Buddhist once remarked, 'Zen is logical — logic isn't!'

Other examples of exchanges between Master and pupil are not so much funny as gruesome. According to one story, a Zen Master, when asked the meaning of Zen, merely raised his right index finger. Subsequently he asked his pupil the same question. When the pupil raised his finger the Master took a knife and cut it off.

The point of these seemingly strange religious practices is often hard to explain in words, for one is meant to grasp the meaning intuitively. Whether stories like this are literally true is not the real point: it is the spiritual truth which is important. One obvious meaning is that enlightenment cannot be expressed verbally. Another point is that nothing should stand between the religious seeker and *satori*, not even the pointing of a finger. The *koan* about the man on the precipice illustrates that if his hands are full of worries, desires or intellectual theories and he is holding on to these, he will never experience what Zen is about: these things must not intervene between the seeker and the experience.

'Sudden' and 'Gradual' Enlightenment

The school of Zen which was founded by Rinzai has stressed the importance of *koans* and codified them, listing some 1700 in number. It is probably because the *koan* has intrigued westerners that we hear much more about Rinzai Zen than about Soto. Yet the two schools are roughly equally represented, and, if anything, Soto dominates slightly in the West.

In Soto Zen, the role of the *koan* is played down. Followers of Soto Zen often criticise the Rinzai school for using artificial means which produce sudden flashes of enlightenment which do not last. After the follower has solved a *koan*, they contend, that person may be no further on, and indeed may have feelings of achievement which instil ideas of the importance of the 'self' — something which, as we have seen, is contrary to the entire teaching of Buddhism. The follower of the Soto path does not need to be given his or her puzzle to solve, for we are all already born with a *koan*. Life itself is a puzzle to which we must find a solution. Why have we been born at all? What is the purpose of human existence? Why is human existence unsatisfactory, and how can we eliminate unsatisfactoriness? To solve the *koan* of human existence, Soto Zen prescribes a more gradual path, consisting almost exclusively of meditation (*zazen*).

Both types of Zen agree that meditation is supremely important. The usual practice is breathing meditation, similar to the kind described in Chapter Five. At various points in the year, Zen Buddhists practice *sesshin* — a meditation retreat in which the amount of meditation builds up as the period progresses. At the beginning of the period (usually about a week) there will be two or three sittings of around half an hour each, building up to a total of five hours in the day as the retreat nears its end.

The Goal of 'No Goal'

In contrast with many other Buddhist traditions, meditation in Zen is usually combined with normal physical activities. The meditative life is accompanied by physical labour, such as tilling the soil to grow vegetables or preparing the food in the kitchen. *Satori* is to be discovered in everyday tasks and not in some special 'other-worldly' religious experience.

Since enlightenment is found in this world, any human activity, performed appropriately, can be a moment of *satori*, whether it is meditating, driving one's car or going about one's daily employment. Books have been written about the relationship between Zen and areas as diverse as archery, flower arranging and social work. Robert Pirsig's book *Zen and the Art of Motorcycle Maintenance* became a best-seller in the mid-1970s and was celebrated for the famous quotation:

> The Buddha, the Godhead, resides quite as comfortably in the circuits of a digital computer or the gears of a cycle transmission as he does at the top of a mountain or in the petals of a flower.[3]

Zen stresses that the follower of the path should be at one with whatever he or she is doing, and fully involved with one's whole true being. One Zen teacher, when asked to summarise Zen, said, 'When you are hungry, eat; when you are thirsty, drink; when you are tired, sleep.' If this seems a banal statement instead of a profound religious ideal, the teachings of Zen cause seekers to enquire whether they really experience a oneness with nature which allows them to eat when they are hungry, drink when they are thirsty and sleep when they are tired. Those who have routine, clock-governed jobs are more likely to eat because it is one o'clock and go to sleep because they have to get up early next morning.

Because *satori* is 'this-worldly' rather than 'other-worldly', Zen Buddhists sometimes say cryptically that the goal is 'no goal'. What they mean is that on enlightenment one does not receive some spectacular supernatural revelation or become transported to some celestial realm. It is *this* world that is seen as it really is. Insofar as it is possible to describe *satori*, a Zen Buddhist will affirm that it is a state of rest, silence and certainty, in which one sees things clearly, with emotion and passion ebbed away; it is a feeling of oneness with the universe, in which distinctions between self and others, and self and the world, are broken down.

The Tea Ceremony

One celebrated practice in which Zen is combined with everyday things is the Japanese tea ceremony — an event which has captured the imagination and interest of westerners. The ceremony originated in China, which is famed for its tea, and was brought to Japan in the twelfth century by a Japanese monk called Eisai who had visited China. The ceremony is still carried out and every April there is a large two-day ceremony — the Great Tea-Offering Ceremony at Saidai-ji.

Many books have been written on the subject of serving tea and there are even several schools of thought about the appropriate way to perform the ceremony. Amongst the most celebrated writings are the *Ch'a Ching* (the colloquial word 'char' in English comes from the Chinese *ch'a*, meaning 'tea'), and Eisai's large two-volume work entitled *Kissa-yojo-ki (Notes on the Curative Effects of Tea)*.

The ceremony began as a religious ritual, where Zen monks solemnly drank tea out of a common cup in front of an image of Bodhidharma. Tea, being a stimulant, also aided the practice of meditation, preventing monks from becoming drowsy during the long *zazen* sessions. According to a legend, Bodhidharma himself found his eyelids closing during meditation, and in his usual ruthless manner cut them off, whereupon they turned into tea leaves!

The tea ceremony has now become secularised, and Bodhidharma's image has been replaced by flowers and a decorative scroll. But some underlying religious ideas can still be seen. The 'tea room', normally separate from one's house, is made of bamboo, suggesting simplicity, naturalness and impermanence. (It is common for a tea house to be pulled down after the tea master's death, rather than to be allowed to endure for a second generation.) The highly formalised ritual is enacted because this is the way one's ancestors performed it.

Since the tea-room is small (normally around ten feet square), the maximum number of guests at any time is five. On arrival the guest waits in the waiting arbour, and, when summoned by the host, proceeds along some stepping stones to a 'crawling entrance' — a small door through which he or she must crawl before reaching the tea room. Guests then remove their sandals. A few small cakes are served and eaten while the host prepares the tea on a brazier, stirring with a whisk to create a froth. The formalities demand that the guest spends time admiring the utensils in a strictly determined order. Even the subjects of conversation are governed by rules: for example, when the utensils are passed round, the chief guest must ask who the craftsmen were, which tea masters approved of them, and so on.

The formalities involved may seem contrary to the spirit of spontaneity which Zen engenders. In origin, partaking of tea was a simple informal activity, and it was only in the sixteenth century CE that over 100 rules were formulated about the appropriate etiquette. Be that as it may, the ceremony still represents the Zen insistence on greatness in simple things. There is no great achievement in tea-drinking, and the utensils are not chosen for any great beauty: indeed equipment is normally selected because of its age rather than its elegance, showing respect for ancient customs and the ancestors who practised them. Highly valuable kettles, ladles or drinking bowls could easily generate the selfish desire which the Buddhist wishes to eliminate. The whole character of the tea ceremony should instil feelings of non-attachment and inner peace.

'Square Zen' and 'Beat Zen'

The notion that Zen can be combined with everyday activities has sometimes been interpreted to mean that 'anything goes' as a possible means for attaining *satori*, whether it is meditating in front of a buddha-image, drinking tea, riding a motorcycle, walking, hitch-hiking, drinking to excess or having an orgy! Zen became interpreted in this way by some westerners when it spread across the United States in the late 1950s. This was the era of the 'beatniks' and many of them found an outlet in Zen for combining their non-conformity with their religious searchings.

Books on Zen began to be produced in abundance around that time, and the 'beat generation' tended to learn about Buddhism through the written word rather than by disciplined study under a Zen *Roshi*. Their form of Zen came to be known as 'Beat Zen', in contrast with the 'Square Zen' of the more serious students who studied under accredited Japanese teachers.

'Beat Zen' attracted some well-known American intellectuals, including poets Gary Snyder and Alan Ginsberg, novelist Jack Kerouac and composer John Cage. In the spirit of Zen, Cage attempted to jolt musical audiences out of their accepted traditional conventions: he achieved fame (or notoriety) by performing at one of his concerts his own composition entitled '4 minutes 33 seconds', at which he sat in complete silence in front of a piano for precisely that length of time. If this was music, it certainly transcended sound!

Kerouac's novel *The Dharma Bums* was a more direct expression of Beat Zen and a fair proportion of it is believed to be autobiographical. Kerouac describes a group of beatniks who travel through the States by hiding amongst the cargo of freight-trains. They experience something of a oneness with nature, often sleeping rough in the open. Their lifestyle consists of smoking cannabis, drinking alcohol to excess when they can afford it, and having casual sexual relationships with partners whom they call 'bodhisattvas'.

Although traditional Zen teachers would not condone the permissiveness of 'Beat Zen', it is easy to see how Zen came to be interpreted in this way. Zen Buddhists undertake to observe Buddhist precepts, but reject slavish conformity, since this can prevent the discovery of one's own buddha-nature. However, finding a middle way between total conformity and complete outlandishness is no easy task for the follower of the Zen path.

One final postscript about Zen may be of interest. Zen Masters are renowned for the tricks they play on each other, in attempts to trap another *Roshi* into putting into words the experience of *satori* which has 'no dependence on words or letters'. 'What do you teach about Zen here?' asked one

Master to a Japanese *Roshi*. To reply in words would be to fall into the trap: the *Roshi* merely lifted his fan and threw it at his questioner.

In the course of writing this book, a Zen priest agreed to read an earlier version of this chapter. As he handed me back the manuscript, he said, 'When you described the "flower sermon", you didn't say what the Buddha passed on to the disciple when he smiled'. I checked what I had written: it seemed clear enough. Then I realised that this was a trap to see if I would put into words the Buddha's sermon of silence. He laughed. 'What I want to know,' he said, 'is — have *you* found it yet?'

Notes to Chapter 6

1 Wu Ch'eng-en, *Monkey* (Unwin Hyman Ltd, 1979) p 316
2 Yoel Hoffman, *The Sound of the One Hand* (Paladin Books, London, 1977) pp 38–40
3 Robert Pirsig, *Zen and the Art of Motorcycle Maintenance* (Corgi, London, 1974) p 18

7

The 'Crown' of Buddhism: Tibet

Tibet Before Buddhism

Buddhism was slow in reaching Tibet, mainly for geographical reasons, the principal problem being the virtual impassibility of the Himalayas, together with a climate to which Indian teachers were quite unaccustomed. Tibet is often described as the 'Land of Snows', it is highly mountainous, being between 13 000 and 16 400 feet above sea level, and in the same season of the year, temperatures can vary between minus 40 degrees Celcius (−40°C) at night and 27 degrees Celcius (+27°C) during the day. When Buddhist teachers finally penetrated Tibetan territory, they discovered that the Tibetans already had their own religions, and it took several centuries for Buddhism to percolate through and to adapt itself. In order to establish itself thoroughly, Buddhism had to undergo a vast transformation and absorb much of the culture and religion that already existed in the country.

Before the advent of Buddhism, the religion practised in Tibet was a form of 'shamanism'. A shaman is an officially appointed priest who is believed to have special powers to communicate with the spirit worlds. By these powers he is able to provide access for mortals to the upper realms of the heavens or the lower realms of the hells. These boundaries could only be linked by the shaman priest who performed special rites, especially at funerals, to close the doors of the tombs by his special powers, and to open up the gates of the celestial abodes. The shaman was not merely a religious figure. In Tibet he also held political power, and together with the king and the chief minister formed a trio with power to govern the region. The king himself was believed to be descended from the upper regions of the heavens and was often regarded as all-knowing and all-wise.

Many features of Tibetan shamanism were absorbed into Buddhism, especially the popular deities. Instead of insisting that the shamanists gave up belief in their deities, skilful Buddhist teachers with supernatural powers performed acts of exorcism, and subdued these gods for the purposes of Buddhism. The role of such deities was, of course, somewhat limited. Tibetans would pray to them for earthly benefits rather than religious ones: as we have seen, Buddhists regard gods as useful for improving affairs in this world but not for enabling men and women to make any kind of spiritual progress.

There were other ways, too, in which traditional Buddhism combined with shamanism. The importance of special funeral rites, for example, finds expression in Tibetan Buddhism in works like *The Tibetan Book of the Dead*. Buddhism reformed many of the ancient Tibetan practices too, particularly by prohibiting animal and human sacrifices.

The 'Crown' of Buddhism

It is not surprising that it was Mahayana Buddhism rather than 'Hinayana' which entered this country. The 'Hinayana' teachers insisted on the importance of sticking very closely to the teachings of the Buddha and the rules of the monastic order. This apparent rigidity made its spread quite impossible in Tibet. In order to sell itself to those of a different persuasion, adaptation was essential. To give one fairly trivial example, 'Hinayana' monks who observed their monastic rules strictly were unable to survive the climate when they only permitted themselves one single robe made of cotton.

Tibetan Buddhism developed a very rich and complicated set of teachings and practices. Often these can only truly be understood by its followers. Even then, they are likely to be familiar only within their own particular form of Tibetan

Buddhism, of which there are many. The rituals are very elaborate and highly symbolic. Much use is made of *mantras* (sacred sounds), *mandalas* (special sacred geometric diagrams), and *mudras* (rather beautiful hand gestures which are used in the course of a meditation). The combination of bodily movement, sound and sight is designed to ensure that in a meditation one's body, speech and mind are all involved: body, speech and mind are the three things which, according to Tibetan thought, make up a person.

Even Buddhists themselves have failed to understand all the complex imagery and symbolism, and have sometimes disparaged Tibetan Buddhism as a debased form of the Buddhist faith, superstitious and obsessed with magic. It is true that disciples will sometimes claim that their teacher has supernatural powers, such as an ability to levitate, or to part the clouds and control the weather. But few accredited teachers make such claims on their own behalf, and any remarkable powers should not distract followers from the true goal of making spiritual progress towards full buddhahood.

Tibetans would certainly not agree that they had reduced the Buddhist religion into a debased form of magic. On the contrary, their form of Buddhism is said to be its 'crown' or the 'flower'. This form of Buddhism is often called the *Vajrayana*, meaning 'Diamond Vehicle'. Some teachers even describe it as 'complete Buddhism'.

In describing itself as the 'Diamond Vehicle', Tibetan Buddhism does not separate itself off from the two traditional vehicles of the Theravada and Mahayana. It claims to combine the ideas of the Hinayana and the Mahayana, and at the same time to add even more, bringing into fruition the religious teachings and practices of these two important forms of Buddhism. From the Hinayana form it derives its basic teachings about morality and the nature of the self: like all other Buddhists, Tibetans acknowledge the Four Noble Truths and the Eightfold Path, as well as the monastic precepts (see chapter 4). From the Mahayana tradition come the profound teachings of many of their scholars and also some of the devotional practices. From the Mahayana they acknowledge the ideal of the bodhisattva and, as we have seen, both Tibetan art and ritual make copious use of various buddha and bodhisattva images.

These images of these buddhas can be presented in a variety of ways: sometimes they are peaceful and serene, like the figures of the Buddha which we see more often in the West, but at other times the buddhas appear extremely fierce, even terrifying in their aspect. This is to demonstrate that a buddha is not someone who meditates passively and makes no difference to the world in which we live; buddhas are very active and fiercely opposed to evil. As well as presenting the buddhas in both their benign and wrathful forms, buddhas and bodhisattvas are portrayed variously as male and female. The female represents *wisdom*, and the male *compassion*. (This contrasts with our western sex-role stereotyping.) In Buddhist art, male and female bodhisattvas are often portrayed in very intimate inter-relationships, to symbolise the close union between wisdom and compassion — the goal which buddhas have attained and to which all should aspire.

Temples and Shrines

Because of the complex symbolism of Tibetan Buddhism, Tibetan temples and shrines are highly complex. Outside a temple in the Tibetan tradition it is common to find prayer wheels (sometimes called prayer mills). A prayer wheel is a wooden cylinder on which prayers are written both inside and outside: a Tibetan Buddhist will rotate the wheel and its prayers as an act of piety. These wheels take the form of large heavy cylinders; but many Tibetans also possess their own personal prayer wheels which are much smaller and are rotated by waving the handle. Prayer wheels are made of wood, gem-studded metal or bone.

Outside the main door of the shrine-room hangs the famous Tibetan Buddhist picture of the 'Wheel of Life'. The Wheel depicts the six realms of existence: humans, animals, gods, asuras, hungry ghosts, and hell-beings. The horrors of

Prayer wheels or mills
Photograph: Stephen Johnson, Media Services, Plymouth Polytechnic.

The wheel of life

the hells are usually portrayed in some detail, since it is important to see how one's karma may work itself out. The Wheel of Life is placed very prominently, since it should be used as a kind of mirror in which one looks at oneself: its position provides a constant reminder that everyone will be reborn in one or other of these realms in one's next rebirth.

The meditation hall is usually large and elaborate inside, with many images of buddhas and bodhisattvas. However, Gautama the Buddha is seldom the central figure. Tibetans of the Nyingmapa (the oldest) tradition, frequently display the image of Padmasambhava, the religious leader who established Buddhism in Tibet, a rather severe figure with a slightly disapproving look! In the Gelugpa (the 'reformed' and established) tradition one might find the bodhisattva Avalokiteshvara (called Chenrezig in Tibet) depicted on a large painted cloth (*thanka*), or a similar portrayal of Manjushri, often regarded as the chief of the bodhisattvas. Other images might include various buddhas (including Gautama), bodhisattvas and well-known scholars from Tibetan religious history. It is a common practice to 'dress' these images. A muslin cloth can be placed around the shoulders of a buddha-image, or a yellow hat on a scholar's head; the scholar can even be provided with a complete set of robes.

Shoes are removed on the threshold and, on entering the meditation hall, worshippers prostrate themselves three times, once for the Buddha, once for the Dharma and once for the Sangha. They then sit in silence on the floor: chairs are used only if a worshipper has some physical disability. If lamas are leading the devotion, they process in, as the members of the congregation stand and bow respectfully to them.

There are many ceremonies for various traditions, occasions and times of the month. I shall describe one which I attended, which gives something of the flavour of Tibetan worship. It was called *Manjushri puja* (the ceremony of devotion to Manjushri), and, after calling on the name of Manjushri, devotees underwent the 'taking of refuge'. This meant affirming their dedication to the Buddha, Dharma and Sangha, and asking that any merit they obtained through the act of devotion might be channelled towards the benefit of

Bodhisattva Manjushri
© *Wisdom Publications. Reproduced by permission.*

all beings who are caught up in the cycle of birth and rebirth. The ceremony lasted for about 45 minutes, alternating between chanting and silence. At one point *mudras* — the rather beautiful hand movements — were used, and various *mantras* were chanted in unison.

Throughout the ceremony, worshippers each used their own small photograph-size picture of Manjushri. These pictures were used for 'visualisation' (see chapter 2). By allowing the image to penetrate the mind, the worshipper aims to become one with Manjushri acquiring the spiritual virtues which are associated with him.

The significance of all the symbolism is not immediately comprehensible. Understanding is something which, I am told, comes gradually, through serious and constant study, and through consistent spiritual practice. For anyone who wants to make spiritual progress, devotional practice and study are seen as completely intertwined. One cannot understand the practice without the necessary learning, nor can one learn without spiritual practice. When I was granted an audience with one of the lamas, I asked what reasons he could give me for accepting the doctrine of karma. I expected an intellectual exchange to commence at this point, but instead I was simply informed that if I engaged in the community's spiritual practices I would in time find that I would come to believe also.

Because learning is a gradual process, a Tibetan teacher will not disclose important teachings to a student until he or she is spiritually ready. The teachings are difficult and in the wrong hands they might be abused or misconstrued. It would therefore be inappropriate, even if it were possible, to present all of the teachings of Tibetan Buddhism. Instead, what follows consists of folk tales about some of Tibet's religious heroes. These are traditions rather than literal historical accounts, but they are tales which are known and loved by most Tibetans.

Some Tibetan Religious Heroes

1 *Padmasambhava*

Padmasambhava is the figure who is sometimes credited with giving Buddhism its first real impetus in Tibet in the eighth century CE. He is venerated by all Tibetan traditions, but particularly by the Nyingmapa sect (the 'Ancient Ones'), which is the oldest Tibetan school. Later traditions, however, have suggested that the folk legends about him have considerably exaggerated his achievements.

The Tibetan Book of the Great Liberation is the principal text which describes the birth and subsequent life of Padmasambhava, and it reads like a gigantic fairy tale. Padmasambhava is said to have been ordained by Ananda (the Buddha's chief disciple) only 12 years after Gautama's death. The book tells us that the birth of Padmasambhava was predicted by Gautama the Buddha himself. As the Buddha lay dying he prophesied that, 12 years later, a lotus blossom would open up in a lake and that out of the flower would appear 'one who will be much wiser and more spiritually powerful than myself. He will be called Padmasambhava'.[1]

The Buddha Amitabha miraculously produced a *stupa* (a shrine) in the lake to which Gautama the Buddha had referred. The king walked around the *stupa* several times, a customary religious act in almost all forms of Buddhism. Suddenly, the predicted lotus blossom appeared in the lake and out of the flower appeared Padmasambhava, seated, in the form of a one year old boy. The boy was brought to the palace, and Amitabha, Avalokiteshvara and ten guardian deities came to him, anointed him with holy water and crowned him as 'the Lotus King'.

As Padmasambhava grew older, he excelled at poetry, philosophy, wrestling, archery, swimming, athletics, astrology, medicine, jewellery, art, carpentry, masonry — indeed every skill one could imagine. But Padmasambhava did not continue to engage in all these worldly pursuits; he began to take up the religious life instead. Because of his religious devotion, he aroused strong opposition and he and his wife, Mandarava, were seized by some of the king's ministers and

Padmasambhava
Permission to reprint courtesy of
Dharma Publishing, Berkeley, CA, USA.

burned at the stake. The king was greatly distressed when he heard of this and went immediately to the site of the funeral pyre. Instead of seeing the ashen remains of Padmasambhava, however, the king beheld a lake with an enormous lotus blossom in the centre, and there, sitting in the middle, were Padmasambhava and Mandarava, completely unscathed. On seeing this miracle, the king and the formerly hostile ministers joined the monastic community and dedicated their lives to Buddhism.

All this, of course, is myth: if it were true, then Padmasambhava would have been around 1200 years old on reaching Tibet, thus putting Methuselah (Gen. 5:27) well and truly in the shade with regard to longevity! But the myth serves to illustrate the high esteem with which Padmasambhava is regarded.

Padmasambhava's appearance in Tibetan history began when King Tritsong Detsen (756–797 CE), a king who advanced the cause of Buddhism, invited a scholar named Shantarakshita from India to spread the Dharma. His mission was initially unsuccessful, for a vast epidemic broke out, as a result of which the king's eldest son died, and there was a great famine. The supporters of shamanism claimed that their gods were angry at the introduction of this alien religion, Buddhism, and mounted a campaign to eliminate it. Because of the calamity which had befallen himself and the Tibetan people, King Tritsong Detsen stated that he had lost confidence in all religions and decreed that the religious leaders would be severely punished if these spirits and demons were not destroyed within seven days.

Although Shantarakshita was a brilliant teacher, he was incapable of pacifying the unrest, coping with the calamities which had befallen Tibet and ensuring that the populace did not abandon the new religion. He therefore felt that a more powerful figure than himself was needed and advised the king to invite Padmasambhava. As we have seen, Padmasambhava had many more skills than Shantarakshita, being not only a scholar, but an accomplished meditator, athlete, and even a magician. Padmasambhava successfully subdued the demons and, together with Shantarakshita, founded the first monastery in Tibet — the famous Samye Monastery — thus putting Buddhism firmly on the map.

The monastery was completed in 787 CE and seven monks were ordained, with a further 300 novices shortly after. Thus the Tibetan Sangha had its beginning. The building was constructed in the shape of a *mandala* and with three storeys — one for each of the three traditional bodies of the Buddha (see chapter 3). The monastery was consecrated, and the king planned the arrival of many translators from India, Nepal, Kashmir and China. (It is said that there were 108 translators in all, which is a sacred number in Tibet.)

Padmasambhava himself is said to have written many religious texts, and 25 *siddhas* (hermit teachers with supernatural powers) hid these in mountains, caves and crevasses: it was now safe to do this since Padmasambhava had subdued the demons who were believed to have inhabited those regions. The texts were to be discovered at a later time by people directed by Padmasambhava, when humankind was in a more spiritually advanced stage to receive these rather difficult teachings. It is believed that texts can lose their power through time and therefore new texts need to be discovered in order to 're-energise' the original teachings. These hidden texts are known as *terma* (*terma* means 'hidden treasure'), and from around 1125 CE onwards several of these texts have been 'found'. Some *terma* are very old, but others were not written by Padmasambhava at all but are probably the work of later thinkers who wished their works to have Padmasambhava's seal of authority upon them. *The Tibetan Book of the Dead* is a *terma* dating from about the fourteenth century.

2   *Milarepa*

Another figure who is much revered is Milarepa (eleventh century CE). Milarepa illustrates how following the Buddhist path can rid oneself of a vast amount of evil karma within a single lifetime. When Milarepa was a child, his father died and his aunt and uncle robbed him of his inheritance. In order to seek revenge, his mother persuaded him to learn black magic to work against the wicked aunt and uncle.

Milarepa
By Sherabpalden Beru. © Kagyu Samye Ling, Tibetan Centre, Eskdalemuir,
Dumfriesshire, Scotland. Reproduced by permission.

Milarepa studied under a renowned black magician and, by working a spell, caused their house to collapse, killing his aunt and uncle, together with other relatives and house guests who had come to celebrate a wedding feast. Thirty-five people died in all. When villagers voiced their suspicions, Milarepa worked a second spell causing a severe hailstorm which destroyed their entire harvest.

Milarepa's fortunes were restored, but he was now a mass murderer and began to feel deep remorse. In repentance he sought out a well-known and uncompromising religious teacher called Marpa. Marpa wanted to test Milarepa's commitment before he would even begin to instruct him in the Dharma. The first task he was given was the construction of a tower in Marpa's grounds. Milarepa set to work and completed the task single-handed, whereupon Marpa informed him that he had changed his mind, and that the tower should be demolished and constructed somewhere else. Milarepa complied and once again Marpa pronounced the same verdict. This happened repeatedly until Marpa had assured himself that Milarepa would do precisely what his teacher instructed; only then did Marpa give him any spiritual training.

Milarepa too became an uncompromising religious character. He spent the greater part of his life meditating in the open air, amid the snow. One of Milarepa's teachings was the 'Doctrine of the Inner Fire', and it is sometimes claimed that meditators like Milarepa were able to melt the snow around them with their inner spiritual energy. Milarepa wore nothing but a white cotton cloth which remained on his body until it fell off with age, after which he meditated naked. On one occasion his cooking pot broke, so instead of finding a replacement Milarepa simply did without one.

Neither Marpa nor Milarepa ever sought ordination as members of the Sangha. Nevertheless, Milarepa is acknowledged as Tibet's greatest *yogi* (meditator) and poet. His teacher, Marpa is the founder of the Kagyupa sect, one of the best-known Tibetan lineages.

3   Atisha

Buddhism went through periods of success and periods of persecution. Three great Tibetan kings (sometimes called the three 'Dharma kings') had lent great support to the Buddhists, but there were constant under-currents of opposition, particularly by the supporters of Tibet's old religion. As a result of a conspiracy, the last of the three great kings was murdered, and his brother Langdarma (who ruled 836–842 CE) occupied the throne. Buddhism almost disappeared: monasteries were destroyed, monks expelled and scriptures burned. Buddhism was revived once more only when the scholar Atisha was brought to Tibet in the eleventh century.

Langdarma was killed in 842 CE by a Buddhist monk, and this event brought about so much rejoicing within the Sangha that it is still commemorated annually by Nyingmapa Buddhists in a special 'Black Hat Dance'. It may seem strange that Buddhists should appear to condone an action which seems so obviously contrary to their fundamental precepts. Nyingmapa Buddhists, however, will justify Langdarma's assassination on the grounds that this prevented him from committing even further misdeeds which would have cast him into the hells for aeons. (This is an isolated example of killing being condoned; although *self*-sacrifice to protect the Dharma became acceptable, especially in the Chinese Mahayana tradition. This was why Vietnamese monks burned themselves to death during the Vietnam War in the 1960s.)

Despite Langdarma's murder, Buddhism was not immediately restored in Tibet. Too much damage had been done, particularly because the Tibetan empire had become so fragmented in the political upheaval which took place. We have no records of what took place in Tibet during the ensuing 150 years, but we know that the scriptures still existed, and this provided a base for the eventual restoration of Tibetan Buddhism.

Buddhism slowly began to revive a generation later under the guidance of King Yesheö of West Tibet. (By this time Tibet had been divided into various regions.) Yesheö abdicated in favour of his nephew in order to become a monk and wanted to bring the renowned scholar Atisha to Tibet. This was to be a costly process, and — so the story goes — Yesheö tried to collect gold, a commodity in which Tibet abounded. In the course of his collecting, Yesheö was captured by a neighbouring Muslim king. He was given a choice: either he could become a Muslim, or he could persuade his subjects to collect his own weight in gold to secure his release. The nephew managed to collect a weight of gold equivalent to that of the king's body, but not enough for the head. He sought an interview with his uncle in captivity to discuss what he ought to do. 'I am now old,' said Yesheö; 'I have done all I can do to further the teachings of the Buddha. Let me die here. Use the gold instead to bring Atisha to Tibet.' Reluctantly, his nephew did so, and when the Muslims saw that the gold was not forthcoming, they beheaded Yesheö. The gold was used to bring Atisha to Tibet.

Atisha (958–1054 CE) came to Tibet from India in 1042 CE and did much to re-establish and reform the teachings which had been spread in Tibet during the first diffusion of Buddhism. Many of these had become confused and distorted in the course of the years and because of the political unrest. Shortly before Atisha's arrival, various magical teachers, and particularly village abbots, engaged in animal sacrifices, had ritual sexual relationships, and even performed magical rituals aimed at causing the death of human beings. No doubt the Buddhists who carried out such actions were vying with the pre-Buddhist shaman priests to show them that the Buddhists had superior magical powers, and because Buddhism was loosely organised, particularly in the villages, these practices had continued unchallenged.

When Yesheö was king he had severely suppressed these activities and Atisha strongly supported these reforms, enforcing the highest standards of morality within Buddhist monasteries. Atisha translated many Indian scriptures: over 100 Indian texts were translated under his guidance. It was as a result of Atisha's tireless activity that Buddhism became firmly established in Tibet and the final victory over the former religion was secured through strict monastic practice and scholarship, rather than by magic.

4 *Tsongkhapa*

Another scholar who is greatly respected is the fourteenth century scholar-saint Tsongkhapa. Buddhists have sometimes said that his achievement was so great that he was like St Thomas Aquinas (the scholar) and St Benedict (saint and monastic reformer) rolled into one! Sometimes he is said to be an incarnation of the bodhisattva Manjushri, and in Tibetan art he sometimes bears Manjushri's sword, lotus and book, together with a yellow hat.

The name 'Tsongkhapa' means 'man from Onion Valley', probably a reference to the region in which the scholar-saint was born (a place called Amdo, now within China). Tsongkhapa was an infant prodigy. His religious education began when he was three, he became a novice monk at the age of seven, and thereafter studied at Tibet's most important seats of learning.

Tsongkhapa founded the famous Ganden monastery near Lhasa, of which he became the first abbot. 'Ganden' means 'paradise'; and it is exquisite, being made of marble, with a gilded roof and the most expensive images installed inside.

Tsongkhapa believed that reforms were needed in the monasteries' discipline. The monks had become lax, abandoning many of their precepts, particularly those relating to marriage, diet, and the observance of retreats; other members of the Sangha had preferred living as hermits to taking part in the monastic life. Tsongkhapa brought many of these hermits back to the monastic communities and not only insisted upon much stricter observance of the monastic precepts, but also emphasised the importance of serious study of Buddhist doctrines. Monks were particularly encouraged to learn logic, and Tsongkhapa instituted great formal debates between them. These were conducted in the presence of a learned and respected abbot, so that the monks would be able to reach conclusions which would be unassailable by the weightiest counter-argument. As a further means of encouraging serious study, Tsongkhapa devised a system of examinations and organised the monks into ranks according to their level of attainment. The highest rank, which still exists today, is the *geshe* (philosopher). Tsongkhapa also encouraged the highly symbolic Tibetan rituals which had developed within the Vajrayana, but many of these were only to be practised by those monks who had first mastered Buddhist doctrine at a sufficiently high level.

To underline the extent of his reforms, Tsongkhapa's followers were made to wear yellow hats on ceremonial occasions, in contrast to the red hats worn by certain other schools. Tsongkhapa's school of the 'yellow hats' became known as the 'Gelugpa', meaning 'virtuous ones'. His nephew, who was one of his pupils, became the first of the Dalai Lamas. Tsongkhapa remains one of the most revered figures within the Gelugpa tradition, and his image will almost always be found in a Gelugpa temple, sometimes even in the chief place.

The Dalai Lama

The best-known figure in the Tibetan tradition is, of course, the Dalai Lama. The western press sometimes refer to him as the 'god-king', but this is inaccurate. He is not a king: although the Potala, his Palace, seems large and grandiose, he merely occupies a very small cell within it. The title 'Dalai Lama' literally means 'ocean teacher' since his wisdom is reckoned to be as vast and as deep as the ocean. However, in spite of his learning, it is not strictly true that he is the 'head' of the Tibetan Buddhists. Matters of doctrine and practice have been determined more usually by the Abbot of Ganden, who is the spiritual leader and focus of the Gelugpa sect — the established school of Tibetan Buddhism before the Communist invasion in 1959. Until the Communist annexation of Tibet, the Dalai Lama was head of state, as well as head of his own monastery in the Potala Palace — the Namgyal Monastery. Although he belongs to the Gelugpa, all Tibetan Buddhists, and indeed most Buddhists throughout the world, respect him and listen to his teaching. He is not a god but is regarded as the incarnation of the bodhisattva Chenrezig (or Avalokiteshvara).

The office of the Dalai Lama is often thought to be a very

ancient tradition, but it only came into being in the sixteenth century CE. The present Dalai Lama — Tenzin Gyatso — is the fourteenth. It is believed that Chenrezig incarnates again after the death of each successive Dalai Lama, and when a Dalai Lama dies, extensive searches are made to find his successor. The dying Dalai Lama may give a prophecy which will help to find his new incarnation. Obviously the time of birth of potential candidates is crucial, and when a likely successor is found, various tests are carried out. The young child who may be destined for this role is required to recognise a certain number of the previous Dalai Lama's belongings, for example, and to have certain memories of his previous life. (A few mistakes are permitted: after all, we can all be mistaken about our memories and belongings in our single present life.) The new Dalai Lama of course will be merely a child and will not be ready to take over the role of leading the monastic community. Until he comes of age, a regent acts on his behalf. The most famous Dalai Lama was the fifth, in whose period of office the construction of the great Potala began.

Could a mistake ever be made about the new candidate's identity? Some Buddhists have suggested that precisely such a mistake was made when the sixth Dalai Lama was appointed. He appeared to be very worldly-minded and often discarded his robes in favour of secular costume, visiting the hostelries of Lhasa and carousing with women. While some Tibetans have their doubts, others hold that the sixth Dalai Lama was using 'skilful means' in spreading the Dharma and was enormously successful in communicating with the people at their own level. He wrote some beautiful love poetry which is still cherished by Tibetans.

The present Dalai Lama lived in the Potala in Lhasa until 1959, when advancing Communist troops forced the inhabitants of most of the monasteries to flee for their lives. The Dalai Lama escaped, disguised as an ordinary monk, and now lives in Dharamsala in Himachal Pradesh (North-West India), where he receives pilgrims and gives teachings. Recently the Chinese invited the Dalai Lama to return to Tibet, which is still annexed to China. He declined to do so, believing that a return might be construed as tacit approval of the present state of political affairs.

Whether there will be a fifteenth Dalai Lama is unclear. It will probably be a long time before the matter is finally decided, since, barring accidents, the Dalai Lama is likely to live for many years, having been born in 1935. Many Tibetans claim to have heard prophecies that the present Dalai Lama will be the last, and many Buddhists would question whether it would make sense to appoint a Dalai Lama outside the environment of Tibet. Incarnate lamas have been discovered outside Tibet, however. Recently the Dalai Lama identified a two-year old Spanish boy as the incarnation of a Tibetan monastery's founder. He was brought to the monastery to take his place as the head. Tibetans are certain that the Dalai Lama will incarnate again somewhere, as indeed he has promised. However, he will not necessarily be reborn as another Dalai Lama and certainly not in Chinese hands.

Note to chapter 7

1   W Y Evans-Wentz (editor), *The Tibetan Book of the Great Liberation* (Oxford University Press, Oxford, 1968) p 105

8

The Short Cut to Nirvana: Pure Land Buddhism

Religious goals are ambitious, often seemingly beyond the reach of ordinary mortals. Particularly when humankind's spirituality seems at a low ebb, pessimism may set in. 'Pure Land' Buddhism took its rise at a time when people's spiritual standards seemed low. Human conditions made it difficult to follow any spiritual path successfully, and nirvana seemed far remote from everyday human life. Why should one wish to take up life as a monk (the Theravadin ideal) when many people were striving instead to make life better on earth? The monastic ideal seemed to devalue life as a lay person. The Buddha had said, 'You yourselves must strive,' yet the effort was surely very great indeed. After all, did not the Buddha himself take at least 530 successive existences before gaining enlightenment under the pipal tree in Bodh Gaya?

From the twelfth century onwards, these were the issues which led some Buddhists in Japan to believe that attaining nirvana was not a live option for the majority of people, and that it would be more realistic to settle for a second-best alternative. In this present life one could lay the foundations for gaining merit which would eventually lead to nirvana, and perhaps one could be reborn in an existence where attaining nirvana would be infinitely easier. Some earlier scriptures, such as the Lotus Sutra (see chapter 9) had indicated that there was a celestial paradise from which one could be directed to nirvana. This 'Pure Land' (or 'Sukhavati', as it is called) was created by the buddhas, and the pilgrim who reached it would have an extremely pleasant sojourn there, and the bodhisattvas would show the devotee the way to nirvana without any further rebirth being necessary. Once the pilgrim reached the Pure Land, nirvana was assured. (The 'Pure Land' is not, of course, nirvana itself, but only a stepping-stone.)

Pure Land Buddhism has sometimes been called 'the school of the short cut' since it seems to offer an easier alternative to rigorous monastic life, involving simple devotion and reliance on a buddha's compassion to make spiritual progress.

The Story of Amitabha

The focus of Pure Land Buddhism is never the historical Buddha Gautama. A number of buddhas are commonly associated with the Pure Land cults, the most popular being the Buddha Amitabha. Unlike Gautama, Amitabha was not a figure in recorded human history. Indeed, the Pure Land scriptures state that he lived *kotis* of years, or several *kalpas* before Gautama. (A *koti* is defined as the number of grains of sand along the banks of the River Ganges, and a *kalpa* is 420 million years: so a historically impossible timescale puts Amitabha outside the realms of human history.)

Pure Land scriptures tell the following story of Amitabha. There was once a monk called Dharmakara who solemnly resolved to become a buddha. He was already familiar with the doctrine of the Pure Land, and asked his teacher, a buddha by the name of Lokeshvararaja, to describe this celestial paradise. It took Lokeshvararaja many years to describe the perfections of the Pure Land and, after listening to this teaching, Dharmakara resolved to create a country which not only possessed the virtues that his teacher had mentioned, but also the excellent qualities of every other buddha-country associated with every past buddha.

The Pure Land which Dharmakara described would contain no hell-beings, no animals, no hungry ghosts, no *asuras* (four of the six realms of rebirth), and would only contain gods and humans. The paradise would be so excellent that these two states (being a god and being a human) would be indistinguishable. There would be no 'falling away'. Once in the Pure Land, there would be no further rebirth before nirvana was reached. The land would contain countless citizens, infinite light, insurpassable quality of life, no misdeeds, and perfect knowledge of the Dharma. Dharmakara continued his speech to describe scented rivers, trees blown by gentle breezes, perfumes, jewels, incense, flowers and music, exotic birds, freedom from all worries and misfortunes, and bodhisattvas continually worshipping the Buddha.

In the course of describing this Pure Land, Dharmakara made a vow. He would not attain enlightenment unless every living being who called on his name was guaranteed citizenship in this buddha-country:

> If those beings who in immeasurable and innumerable buddha-countries, after they have heard my name, when I shall have obtained Bodhi [enlightenment], should direct their thought to be born in that buddha-country of mine, and should for that purpose bring their stock of merit to maturity, if these should not be born in that buddha-country, even those who have only ten times repeated the thought (of that buddha-country), barring always those beings who have committed the (five) unpardonable sins, and who have caused an obstruction and abuse of the good Law, then may I not obtain the highest perfect knowledge.[1]

(The five 'unpardonable' misdeeds in Buddhist thought are: killing one's father, killing one's mother, killing an arhat, shedding the blood of a buddha, and causing schism in the Sangha. One important Pure Land scripture suggests that entry into the Pure Land is impossible after such misdeeds. Other Pure Land scriptures, however, are more lenient and suggest that cardinal offenders can still obtain nirvana by invoking Amitabha's assistance, but with infinitely greater difficulty.)

As Dharmakara made his vow, the earth began to tremble, hundreds of musical instruments were heard in the sky, sandalwood was scattered from the heavens, and a loud voice exclaimed, 'You will be a buddha in this world'. So Dharmakara became the Buddha Amitabha ('Amitabha' means 'possessing infinite light'). Dharmakara's vow was that he would not become a buddha unless every living being was born in his Pure Land; therefore devotees of Amitabha expect not only that they themselves will be reborn in his paradise, but that everyone who calls upon his name will reach it and be shown the way to nirvana.

Invoking Amitabha

Although Pure Land Buddhism had its hey-day in eleventh century Japan, it first gained ground in China. A Buddhist teacher by the name of Shan-tao (seventh century) was himself believed to be an incarnation of Amitabha. He distributed many copies of the Pure Land Sutra, and wrote a commentary on it which recommended *nembutsu*, the practice of calling on Amitabha's name. He also taught that followers should chant the *sutras* (scriptures), meditate on the Buddha, and worship him by means of buddha-images in shrines.

Shan-tao's work inspired a Japanese monk called Honen (1133–1212 CE), who was the founder of the Jodo school. ('Jodo' is Japanese for 'Pure Land'.) Honen wrote a popular treatise, believing that Buddhism was not for monks only, but that ordinary men and women too should be able to understand enough Buddhist teaching to obtain liberation. Honen taught that, by and large, traditional scriptures were too difficult for the average lay person to understand. But the grace of Amitabha was so great that the gaining of liberation need not depend on understanding the complexities of Buddhist philosophy. The *sutras* he said, were unnecessary: only devotion was required. Constantly repeating the name of Amitabha was sufficient. When other monks saw Honen's popular book, they were so disgusted with it that they burned as many copies as they could find, but this did not prevent the spread of Jodo Buddhism.

Another famous Pure Land teacher was Shinran, a disciple

of Honen. Shinran's sect is sometimes called Jodo Shinshu, the 'True Pure Land Sect'. His is the most popular form of Pure Land Buddhism in Japan today, having 13 million followers, in contrast with Jodo, which has only around 4 million. There are other minor Jodo sects in Japan, only sustaining a following of a few thousand each.

Shinran was a monk who deliberately discarded his robe and refused to shave his head, in order to show that people did not have to follow the monastic life to attain nirvana. He also married and had children. He preferred to preach in Japanese villages, rather than in the towns, so that simple people would also hear his message. In contrast to Honen, he claimed that any attempt to gain merit through good deeds was futile, for devotion alone brought merit. Evil people as well as good ones would be welcomed to Amitabha's Paradise, provided that they called upon his name, even if they only remembered to do this at the moment of their death. Unlike Honen, Shinran denied that it was necessary to repeat constantly the name of Amitabha. One repetition (*nembutsu*) of 'Namu-Amida-Butsu' would suffice; if one repeated Amitabha's name more often, then this could be done in praise of Amitabha for his great benevolence to all living beings. But these further repetitions did not serve to make his Pure Land any easier to gain, or to enhance its benefits.

One further Pure Land teacher deserves mention. Ippen was a wandering teacher who recommended set times of the day — six in all — for chanting the *mantra* 'Namu-Amida-Butsu'. His sect is called the Ji-shu, or 'Times' school. It still exists but attracts only a few thousand followers.

Distortion or development?

Opponents of Pure Land Buddhism often claim that this particular Buddhist path is a distortion of the original teachings of the Buddha. After all, did not the Buddha teach self-effort, and not liberation through some super-human figure like Amitabha? Did not the Pure Land schools substitute devotion for meditation, when the latter brought Gautama the Buddha to enlightenment? Was not the Buddha's emphasis on gaining 'perfect view', dispelling ignorance and desire, rather than on devotion? Surely the Buddhist should concentrate on eliminating desire rather than aspiring to a celestial country where all desires are satisfied? One western writer goes so far as to suggest that Pure Land Buddhists are as true to orthodox Buddhism as the Jehovah's Witnesses are to Christianity.

This last comparison is unjust. In terms of sheer numbers, Pure Land was the most popular form of Buddhism in Japan before the Second World War, only to take second place with the revival of the Nichiren sects (see chapter 9). It is not particularly useful to decide whether Pure Land is 'pure Buddhism' or 'true Buddhism'. It is possible that non-Buddhist influences helped to cause its development. Possibly the plurality of buddhas derives from Hindu devotion where it is common practice to worship many forms of God, and the constant chanting of the name of Amitabha may come from the Hindu practice of invoking the gods in this way (called *japa*). However, all religions adapt and absorb the ideas of surrounding cultures. Pure Land is one example within Buddhism, but Tibetan Buddhism, Zen and Nichiren are equally examples of the same occurrence.

To say that Pure Land Buddhism substituted devotion for meditation is not quite accurate. To focus one's mind on Amitabha is a form of meditation, and we have already seen how visualising a buddha or a bodhisattva is considered a meditative practice (see chapter 5). Some Pure Land Buddhists also taught that there was great value to be gained in meditating not merely on a buddha-image, but on good works themselves. In fact, one cannot separate devotion and deeds. Those who are truly devoted to Amitabha will not commit misdeeds: the Pure Land scriptures clearly state that, although Amitabha receives all men and women to his paradise, whether they are good or evil, those who have committed evil deeds will find nirvana infinitely more difficult to attain than those who have practised the Dharma and observed the precepts. Indeed, one cannot meditate on

Amitabha without acquiring some of the virtues, such as compassion, which he represents. The idea of 'transference of merit' (performed by Amitabha) is quite consistent with traditional Buddhism also. If there are no 'selves', it cannot be right for me to try to gain nirvana for 'myself' — I must equally be concerned with all living beings attaining nirvana, as indeed Dharmakara was when he made the famous vow which enabled him to become the Buddha Amitabha.

I do not think it is true to say that the Pure Land is presented as a place where all desires are fulfilled, and that the notion contradicts the Buddha's teaching about 'non-attachment'. The scriptures carefully qualify the statement about fulfilling desires: all desires are fulfilled, but, they state, 'according to the *Dharma*'. This makes an enormous difference: in the Pure Land, one's requests are not granted, come what may; they are granted if they are in accordance with the teaching of the Buddha. A pilgrim who has reached the Pure Land should not expect to ask for great riches and receive them immediately; what the sincere pilgrim must desire is spiritual benefit — to be shown the path to full nirvana, which lies beyond the Pure Land.

Certainly, there are enormous differences between Pure Land and Theravada Buddhism. Gautama the historical founder is clearly less important to the Pure Land Buddhists than is Amitabha, or whatever Buddha acts as the focus of devotion. But if the life of a Theravada monk is more demanding than Pure Land devotion, the Pure Land Buddhist would see this as a virtue and not a vice. What is wrong with a spiritual short cut? If one is making a journey it is senseless to take a longer route than is necessary. Pure Land Buddhists believe that it is because of the Buddha's compassion that this easier path is shown. Indeed Shinran believed that Pure Land did not offer the shorter route, but the *only* route, since humankind was living in an age where spiritual development was impossible. If a Buddhist wants to attempt a more stringent set of spiritual practices, that person is welcome to do so; but Pure Land claims to offer the simplest means of reaching the goal.

Note to Chapter 8

1   'Larger Sukhavati-Vyuha Sutra' (8.19) from E B Cowell (editor) et al, *Buddhist Mahayana Texts* (New York/Dover, 1969) part II, p 15

9

The Lotus of the True Law:
Nichiren and his Followers

We have seen how Buddhism adopted different forms as it came into contact with different religions and cultures. Buddhism underwent a further transformation in Japan, as a result of the teachings of Nichiren, a thirteenth century Buddhist prophet. Today Nichiren Buddhism is the most popular version of Buddhism in Japan, and we shall explore some of its forms in this chapter.

Although Nichiren Buddhism is so popular, it is often seriously neglected. This is no doubt because it is such a controversial movement, and many Buddhists from other traditions question its credentials to be Buddhism at all. Yet the Nichiren Shoshu sect has about as large a membership in the United Kingdom as the Buddhist Society of Great Britain, which spans every Buddhist tradition.

Nichiren Buddhism began to rise in the twelfth century CE, and has undergone a major revival in the last century. It is best known in the form of the Soka Gakkai, its lay wing. Nichiren Buddhism has now spread to the West, and it is one of the most popular forms of Buddhism taken up by westerners. Nichiren Buddhists base their teachings on an ancient Mahayana Buddhist scripture called the *Lotus Sutra*.

First encounters

I first encountered a Nichiren Buddhist on a train journey. A young woman sitting opposite me was deeply engrossed in a small red booklet entitled *The Liturgy of Nichiren Shoshu*, obviously vocalising the words she was reading under her breath. When she had finished I asked her about her faith. She had been chanting part of the Lotus Sutra the required number of times for the day, which she had now finished doing. In addition to reciting the scripture, she and her fellow-Buddhists regularly chanted the *mantra*, 'Nam myoho renge kyo', a very powerful form of words which is believed to sum up the whole of that scripture, and indeed all of Buddhism. The *mantra* is used to bring about solutions even to everyday problems which one encounters. A sick person can use the *mantra* to effect a cure; someone who is impoverished may chant to procure wealth; someone who lacks a partner of the opposite sex may chant in order to find one. In the case of the young woman opposite me, she often felt uneasy about making long journeys and had hoped that someone would speak to her as she travelled. She had chanted about this and regarded my approach as a favourable outcome of her chanting.

I subsequently attended a small local Nichiren Shoshu ceremony called a *gongyo*. ('Nichiren Shoshu' means 'Orthodox Nichiren Sect'.) The average meeting has about a dozen members, constituting a 'chapter'. A stranger might have been forgiven for wondering what the ceremony had to do with Buddhism. It was a lay group: there were no priests and no monks in saffron robes. There was no image of the Buddha, no 'taking refuge' in the Triple Gem, and no reference was made to the Precepts, the Noble Truths or the Eightfold Path. For the most part, the congregation chanted the words of the small red book in Japanese several times over, following this with the famous *mantra*, 'Nam myoho renge kyo'. Like most other Buddhist ceremonies, however, incense was used, and we were seated on meditation cushions. In place of a buddha-image, the focus of attention was a small black cabinet in a corner (called a *butsudan*) containing a *gohonzon*. A *gohonzon* is a scroll which is inscribed by the High Priest and, in order to receive one, a follower must have been a member for approximately a year. It is difficult to obtain; it cannot be made by oneself and it is not permissible

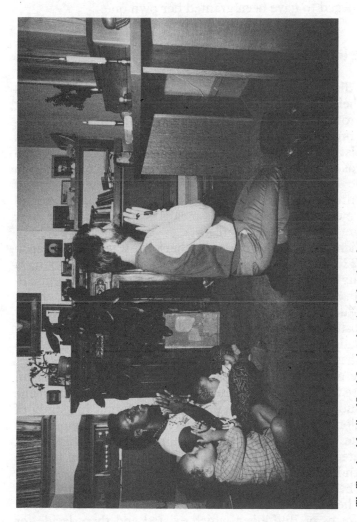

The Trenchard family of South London chanting before the gohonzon
Photograph: Clive Bartlett. © NSUK. Reproduced by permission.

even to reproduce a picture of one. If the owner leaves the order or dies, the *gohonzon* must be returned to the Japanese headquarters. The owner of this *gohonzon* therefore felt very privileged to have been granted her own one.

The life of Nichiren

The distinctive practices of the Nichiren sects can be traced to their founder, Nichiren, who was probably the most controversial figure in the history of Buddhism. His followers claim that he discovered the one true form of Buddhism amidst all the other erroneous forms, while his critics brand him as a fanatic and a demagogue: comparison has even been made between Nichiren and Adolf Hitler! Followers of Nichiren Shoshu call their founder 'Nichiren Daishonin' (*dai* means 'great' and *shonin* means 'sage'), and never refer to him baldly as 'Nichiren'.

Nichiren, the son of poor fisherfolk, was born in Japan in 1222. The name 'Nichiren' was an assumed name (*nichi* means 'sun', and *ren* 'lotus'); his given name being Zennichimaro. At the age of 11, the young Zennichimaro was sent to be educated to the temple called Seicho-ji, high on Mount Kiyosumi. This temple belonged to the Tendai sect, a form of Buddhism which has similarities to Zen, but which also emphasises the Lotus Sutra. Later, the Seicho-ji absorbed some of the ideas and practices of Pure Land Buddhism. There were so many different ideas going around in the name of Buddhism that Nichiren Daishonin found his study of religion very confusing. However, he adopted the practices of the Jodo school, a form of Pure Land Buddhism, and chanted the name of the Buddha Amitabha — a practice which he bitterly regretted later in life.

When he was 16 he entered the priesthood and two years later he left the Seicho-ji. He resolved that he would study all the forms of Buddhism which existed and then decide for himself which was correct. He spent 13 years travelling and studying under the most prestigious teachers in Japan. Having studied all the major schools of Buddhism, Nichiren

Daishonin concluded that the Lotus Sutra was the only true doctrine for the age and that all other teachings were unsuitable for the era in which he lived. Not only did Nichiren Daishonin claim that the Lotus Sutra enshrined the truly authentic teachings of Buddhism, but the preaching of the Lotus Sutra, he taught, was the real and only reason why Gautama the Buddha had appeared on earth.

Early one morning in 1253, Nichiren Daishonin, now 31 years old, climbed to the top of a hill at Kasagamori, overlooking the Pacific Ocean, and, as the sun rose, chanted in a loud voice, 'Nam myoho renge kyo'. Nichiren Daishonin had proclaimed that this was the correct way to practise Buddhism in the present age.

'Myoho renge kyo' is the Chinese title of the Lotus Sutra, which Nichiren Daishonin accepted, and *nam* is a Sanskrit word meaning 'homage to'. The *mantra* is not only the title of the Lotus Sutra but, Nichiren Daishonin taught, encapsulates the entire essence of this scripture. As Nichiren Daishonin taught:

> ... included within the title, Nam-myoho-renge-kyo, is the entire sutra consisting of all eight volumes, twenty-eight chapters and 69 384 characters without exception.[1]

Nichiren Daishonin's conclusion that the Lotus Sutra enshrined the true essence of Buddhism met with a very unfavourable reception. The Zen Buddhists could not accept the Lotus Sutra, since they claimed that enlightenment was gained through a special transmission outside the scriptures. The Pure Land Buddhists said that the Lotus Sutra was too difficult to be taught and objected to the fact that it focussed on Gautama, the historical Buddha, rather than the Buddha Amitabha, who was their focus of devotion.

The Burning Building, the Magic City and the Treasure Tower

To find out why Nichiren Daishonin held that Lotus Sutra was of such paramount importance we must say something about what the Lotus Sutra teaches.

Many Buddhist scriptures have a storyline and the Lotus Sutra is no exception. It tells how the Buddha, during his lifetime, preached to a large audience consisting of lay devotees, monks, nuns, arhats and bodhisattvas. There is even a tradition amongst some Nichiren Buddhists that Nichiren Daishonin himself was one of the principal bodhisattvas who listened to the Buddha; although he was not born as a human until the twelfth century, he attended in a celestial form. (The Nichiren schools view the story as historically true, while modern Buddhist scholars hold that the Lotus Sutra is a fairly late text, written possibly around 250 CE.) Asked to preach the Dharma, the Buddha requested his hearers to regard all his previous teachings as provisional only, for he had not given them the full and final truth: they should not be content to achieve nirvana but should go beyond it, to become full celestial buddhas. The Sutra records that, on hearing this, 5000 members of his audience walked out, disgusted with the teaching. We are to understand that they represented the Hinayana Buddhists who believed that their teachings were already complete.

The Buddha stated that, contrary to popular belief, he did not gain enlightenment under the pipal tree during his earthly life: he had been enlightened many ages previously and only seemed to escape from samsara to nirvana as a skilful device for teaching humankind. In the past, said the Buddha, he only gave provisional teachings, since he taught at the level at which people were situated. Although on the surface this may seem deceptive, the Buddha used two parables to suggest that this was not so.

The first parable is about a burning building. A wealthy housekeeper had a house with a thatched roof and only one door. This house suddenly became ablaze. The householder made for the door, but was unable to persuade his children to come since they were too absorbed in their games. In order to induce them to come, he employed a skilful device and offered them expensive animal-drawn carts to play with if they came. They followed him, and, once outside, demanded their presents. Being wealthy, the householder bought them the most expensive cart he could afford, far exceeding their expectations. The point of the parable is that the Buddha now offers the 'best vehicle', which (we are to understand) is the Mahayana form of Buddhism, claiming it to be far superior to the paths offered by the Hinayana.

Another parable of the Lotus Sutra, although not stressed so much by Nichiren Buddhists, tells of a party of monks in a vast forest, looking for the great Isle of Jewels. They had a guide who was well acquainted with the difficult forest and who was well able to escort them. However, the journey was long, and the monks began to tire and complain; they wanted to turn back because the journey seemed too difficult. Not wishing the monks to return, the guide conjured up a magic city in which they could spend the night, and then go on once they were rested. However, faced with the delights of the magic city, the monks thought that they had reached the end of their destination and did not want to proceed any further. Once they were suitably refreshed, however, the guide miraculously caused the magic city to disappear, so that the monks would resume their quest for the Isle of Jewels, which was more desirable by far.

The magic city represents the 'lesser vehicle' (Hinayana) and the Isle of Jewels the 'greater' (Mahayana). Just as it was not dishonest of the guide to offer the travellers the magic city before they arrived at the Isle of Jewels, so it was not wrong for the Buddha to offer the 'provisional' teachings which the 'Hinayana' enshrined. Yet it is important to recognise that there are greater treasures in store, just as the characters in the parables should have recognised that safety was more important than their games and that the Isle of Jewels was more desirable than the magic city.

As the Buddha continued his preaching a large *stupa* (monument) arose from the earth and became suspended in the sky. It was made of precious materials and decorated with flowers, arches, banners and garlands of jewels. From this treasure tower a loud voice was heard, saying, 'Excellent, excellent! You, Shakyamuni, the World-Honoured One, have expounded the Sutra of the Lotus Flower of the Wonderful Law. Thus is it, thus is it! What you, Shakyamuni, the World-Honoured One, have expounded is all true.'[2]

Shakyamuni (Gautama) opened the middle door of the tower, where a second buddha, called Taho, was seen seated cross-legged on his throne. (Taho is the Japanese name; in Sanskrit he is called Prabhutaratna.) Taho asked Gautama to join him and Gautama entered and sat down at Taho's right hand.

The point of the vision is that it is possible for more than one Buddha to exist in each age — a distinctive Mahayana view. A Buddha after death is not 'beyond recall' but continues to reveal himself to give teachings which are suitable for the level which humankind has reached.

Exile and Execution

These are the highlights of the scripture which Nichiren Daishonin regarded as supreme. Nichiren Daishonin believed not only that the Lotus Sutra was true but that it had power to cope with all calamities and disasters. At the time of Nichiren Daishonin's preaching, Japan had been plagued by all kinds of misfortunes. There had been earthquakes, typhoons, floods, droughts, famines and epidemics. The Mongols, who had conquered Korea under Kubla Khan (himself a Vajrayana Buddhist), now threatened Japan. Nichiren Daishonin went to the crossroads at Kamakura (the year was 1260) and preached that the condition of the country could only be improved by accepting the Lotus Sutra as the one true teaching for the age and that all other forms of Buddhism should be banished from Japan.

Because of his forthrightness, Nichiren Daishonin received much persecution during his lifetime. He was exiled on two occasions, once to the Izu Peninsula and once to Sado Island off the north coast of Japan. He was once sentenced to execution, and, it is said, only managed to escape by a remarkable miracle. Nichiren Daishonin, seated on the execution mat, uttered the *mantra* 'Nam myoho renge kyo', and tilted his head forward in anticipation. Suddenly a brilliant flash of light burst across the sky, blinding the executioner and causing total confusion. Some of the execution party fled, some prayed and others hid in terror. 'Here, why do you shrink from this miserable prisoner?' cried Nichiren Daishonin to the executioner. 'Come nearer! Come closer!' But the execution could not proceed.

Nichiren Daishonin's Transformation

Different Nichiren sects give different accounts of the status of Nichiren within their tradition. According to the Nichiren Shoshu, the remainder of Nichiren Daishonin's story runs as follows. The escape from execution (12 September 1271) was a rebirth of Nichiren Daishonin, who became markedly transformed after this experience. According to his followers, his change was not to be explained by an adverse reaction to the trauma, or as a mere change of policy: Nichiren Daishonin was now ready to proclaim who he really was. He was the primal eternal Buddha, who had been in the universe for as long as it had existed and long before Gautama the Buddha lived on earth. He was as eternal as the sacred law of 'Nam myoho renge kyo'. Nichiren Daishonin's teaching until now had been a mere shadow of the complete truth.

As a Buddha, Nichiren Daishonin himself was worthy of veneration. Nichiren Daishonin therefore devised an object of worship which would incorporate the *mantra* 'Nam myoho renge kyo', together with his own name, since both he and the law had existed from all eternity. This was the *gohonzon*, which is used today in the *gongyo* ceremony. As Nichiren Daishonin said:

> I, Nichiren, have inscribed my life in ink, so believe in the *gohonzon* with your whole heart.[3]

These first *gohonzon* were personally inscribed by Nichiren Daishonin, and some still exist today. *Gohonzon* means 'worthy object of devotion' and it represents the treasure tower which the Lotus Sutra describes. As well as the characters 'Nam myoho renge kyo' and Nichiren Daishonin's name, the *gohonzon* contains the names of Shakyamuni (Gautama), Taho and other figures mentioned in the Lotus

Sutra, written in large ink characters. As the worshipper faces the *gohonzon*, he or she is looking at the treasure tower of 'Nam myoho renge kyo'.

Three Secret Laws

The *gohonzon* was connected with 'Three Great Secret Laws' revealed by Nichiren Daishonin. The *first* is the invocation, 'Nam myoho renge kyo'; the *second* is the 'Dai-Gohonzon'; and the *third* is the place of worship, the construction of which Nichiren Daishonin entrusted to his followers.

We have already explained 'Nam myoho renge kyo'. We must now say something about the *Dai-Gohonzon*. *Dai gohonzon* means 'supreme object of worship' and refers to the *gohonzon* personally inscribed by Nichiren Daishonin in gold characters upon black lacquer and carved by his disciple and successor, Nikko. It is made for all humankind, and on the right it reads, *'ichiembudai soyo'*, meaning 'bestowed upon the entire world'. Its function is to enable people to find peace and prosperity. The *Dai-Gohonzon* is now to be found at the Nichiren Shoshu Head Temple at Taiseki-ji, at the foot of Mount Fuji. Around two million pilgrims find their way there each year from Japan and elsewhere. Nichiren Daishonin also inscribed other *gohonzon*, which he gave to individual followers.

When Nichiren Daishonin died in 1282, his leadership passed to six main disciples, one of whom was Nikko. According to the Nichiren Shoshu, the other five misunderstood Nichiren Daishonin's teaching and, fearing persecution after his death, reverted to Tendai Buddhism. Whatever happened, there was a dispute which Nikko lost, and he felt that he had no option except to leave. He departed, taking with him the *Dai-Gohonzon*, Nichiren Daishonin's writings, and the ashes of his cremated body. In Taiseki-ji, he constructed the Dai-bo, which became the head Nichiren Temple. The Nichiren Shoshu school claims to be in direct lineage to Nikko and that it is the only sect to preach the Buddhism of Nichiren Daishonin, the only true teaching of the eternal law of 'Nam myoho renge kyo'. Other Nichiren schools concede that Nikko took away a *gohonzon* inscribed by Nichiren, but claim that this was only one of several.

Enlightenment through Desire

Nichiren Shoshu also holds that there is a principle by which earthly desires can be changed into enlightenment through chanting 'Nam myoho renge kyo'. As Nichiren said, 'Those who believe in the Lotus Sutra will gather fortune from ten thousand miles afar'.[4]

There are two sides to one's nature: *bonno* (evil desires) and enlightenment. But the two cannot be separated. Desire is not totally evil: it is inherent in human nature to have desires (for example, for food, sleep and sex). Nichiren Shoshu believes the Pure Land schools to be mistaken in supposing that there is a celestial paradise which is totally good, contrasting with the physical world which is unsatisfactory. *Bonno* and enlightenment are inseparable:

> If the minds of the people are impure, their land is also impure, but if their minds are pure, so is their land. There are not two lands, pure and impure in themselves. The difference lies solely in the good or evil of our minds.[5]

It is rather like the lotus flower and the muddy swamp. The swamp needs the lotus flowers if it is to have any semblance of beauty; but, equally, the lotus needs the swamp if it is to grow at all. The Buddha, whom we should strive to become, must come out of the swamp of desire, yet be the beautiful bloom of the lotus. This is why the Nichiren Shoshu justifies chanting in order to acquire health, money, or friends. As their present international leader explained:

> New members start chanting because they want to solve their problems or to fulfil their desires. However, if you read the Daishonin's writings more deeply, you will understand that this is not the ultimate reason for our faith.[6]

If men and women turned to the Lotus Sutra, it is said, they would see that the source of their suffering is their earthly desires and that this world is potentially a paradise. The practical values of worldly gain and material satisfaction are to be pursued just as much as goodness and beauty. This teaching implies that one should not renounce the physical world in the quest for a state of nirvana which is different; nor should one seek a Pure Land which contrasts with an impure one. Nichiren Shoshu is world-affirming, and Buddhists of this school have great concern for preserving human life, for protecting the environment, and for furthering the cause of peace. Nirvana must not be found anywhere else but in this world.

The Eternal Cycle

All this seems very different from the teachings of Gautama the Buddha. Where, one might ask, are the Noble Truths, the Eightfold Path and the precepts? Did not the Buddha teach the elimination of unsatisfactoriness, whereas the Nichiren Shoshu teaches enlightenment through earthly desires and the sufferings which go with them?

Buddhists of the Nichiren Shoshu sect claim that the cycle of birth, old age, sickness and death (the last three being three of the Buddha's four 'encounters' which made him leave the palace) *is* enlightenment. It is to be remembered that, according to the Lotus Sutra, Gautama was already enlightened before his birth on earth. Even a Buddha is not free from this cycle, and can expect to be reborn: chanting 'Nam myoho renge kyo' is a means of coming to terms with eternal rebirth, and not a means of escape from it. Members can chant about their next rebirth, and often do: interestingly enough, many often express a desire to have similar sufferings in their next existence, and not a rebirth in some earthly paradise.

For the Nichiren Shoshu Buddhist, life simply goes on indefinitely, without any final goal. It is not expected that all will attain a nirvana from which there is no return, nor that all living beings will inhabit a Pure Land from which there will be no 'falling away'. Even the goal of universal world peace, at which Nichiren Shoshu aims, is seen as a fragile state of affairs. Once universal peace is attained, humankind's basic vices will still be there — ignorance, greed and hatred (the traditional Buddhist trio). However, humans can expand their capacity to deal with these, and this comes through chanting. One's behaviour is controlled by chanting the *mantra*, not by observing any set of monastic or lay precepts. Nichiren Buddhists explain that there are no precepts as such, for all the precepts that are needed are already contained in the *mantra* 'Nam myoho renge kyo'.

The Soka Gakkai

Nichiren Buddhism had a revival from the mid-nineteenth century onwards, and emerged afresh in various forms. During the period 1930–1945, some Nichiren sects were fervently nationalistic and some even wanted all the countries of the East to unite under the control of Japan. Nichiren Shoshu resisted the pressures of militaristic government, with the result that the lay society (Soka Gakkai) was banned and its leaders imprisoned. However, the experiences of Hiroshima and Nagasaki caused extreme nationalism to give place to an emphasis on peace and brotherhood.

Of all the various forms of Nichiren Buddhism the most prominent and fastest growing is the Soka Gakkai. It is vigorous—some have said aggressive—and is now a worldwide organisation. Members of the Soka Gakkai often draw attention to its growth between 1955 and 1968, when membership mushroomed from 348 160 to 15 729 636—an expansion by a multiple of 45! The Komeito ('clean politics') Party is the political organisation which is comprised of Nichiren Shoshu members. It has heavily influenced trade unions and has gained many political victories.

The Soka Gakkai was founded in 1930 and was dedicated to educational research and the extension of the Nichiren Shoshu. Its leaders have great evangelical zeal and advocate the practice of *shakubuku*. This means, literally, 'break and subdue': the resistance of a non-adherent is to be broken down, not by physical force, but by forceful debate. Buddhists of this sect insist that *shakubuku* is to be understood more in the sense of encouraging or inviting rather than relentless brow-beating. In non-Buddhist countries their methods of spreading the message is called *shoju*, which means 'planting' or 'instilling'. By these means, Nichiren Shoshu has spread abroad to countries including Great Britain and the USA.

Other Nichiren Sects

A number of smaller groups have derived their teachings and practices from Nichiren. Members of the Nichiren Shoshu view the other Nichiren groups as having fallen away from the true teachings of Nichiren Daishonin and, specifically, as having down-graded Nichiren Daishonin's true status. For the Nichiren Shoshu, Nichiren Daishonin is the eternally existent Buddha (the 'adi-Buddha'), while the other schools, they say, view him as no more than a bodhisattva.

This accusation is partly true: other Nichiren schools do speak of the 'bodhisattva Nichiren'. However, the question of whether Nichiren Daishonin is the eternal Buddha or a bodhisattva does not seem as important to them as it does to the Nichiren Shoshu, and they are not so inclined to regard their different characteristics as the result of any dispute about doctrines. When I recently spoke to a monk of the Nipponzon Myohoji sect (a Nichiren order), he swiftly dismissed my questions about Nichiren as unimportant and refused to give an answer. What was important to him was the goal of world peace which the order was promoting.

Reiyukai

It is appropriate to say something about these other Nichiren sects. The Reiyukai emerged from within the Nichiren tradition in 1919, and, like Nichiren Shoshu, followers lay great emphasis on the Lotus Sutra. They use their own particular abridged version, called the 'Blue Sutra': this was compiled by their founder, Kakutaro Kubo (1892–1944), and consists of short passages from the Lotus Sutra together with a few other Buddhist scriptures.

Reiyukai's western literature invites the seeker to a spiritual journey called 'inward self-development', a quest to find one's true self. To discover the inner self, we must realise that we are the products of our past, and in particular the attitudes, beliefs and actions of our ancestors. This is why it is considered important to establish links with our ancestors: establishing such links is reckoned to help us see their effects on our everyday lives and on humankind as a whole. Ancestor remembrance also serves to establish links with the rest of humanity: since each child has two parents, a link with eight generations of ancestors is effectively a link with at least 64 individuals and no doubt a lot more; a link with 20 generations creates a link with over 1 480 000 other individuals.

To remember someone we normally need some token of remembrance, such as a photograph, some keepsake, or even some piece of information about that person. Since it is not always possible to have such reminders, Reiyukai members focus their devotion on a paper scroll on a wooden stand: this is called a *sokaimyo*, which is inscribed with ink characters representing the names of their ancestors.

Ancestor remembrance is not merely an attempt to look back into the past. It enables followers of Reiyukai to understand more fully how they fit into the 'flow' of the rest of humanity, and how they are to 'open their destiny', via their ancestors, to the future. The name 'Reiyukai' means 'Spiritual Friendship Society', and members stress the oneness of humankind through ancestor remembrance.

Others are to be encouraged in the right direction too, and, like the Nichiren Shoshu, Reiyukai Buddhists seek to increase their numbers. They prefer to call their winning of converts *michibiki* ('encouragement') rather than the more aggressive-sounding *shakubuku*. Membership, they explain, does not demand giving up one's current religion, and they have no objection to a member claiming also to be a mainstream Christian. (Mainstream Christians, on the other hand, may not be so willing for Christianity to be combined with Reiyukai practices.) Membership involves paying a modest monthly subscription (Reiyukai do not accept donations) and reciting the Blue Sutra daily.

Rissho-Kosei-kai

In 1938, a break-away group emerged from the Reiyukai, led by two of its members, Niwano Nikkyo (born in 1906), a Tokyo businessman, and Naganuma Myoko (1899–1957), a housewife. Niwano's daughter and Naganuma were both believed to have been cured of illnesses as a result of spiritual healing performed by the Reiyukai and this prompted them to become actively involved in the movement. However, a Reiyukai leader publicly denounced Niwano for practising divination, and Niwano promptly left, accompanied by Naganuma and around 30 others. They formed a separate group which became known as the Rissho-Kosei-kai (meaning 'Society for Establishing Righteousness and Friendly Relations').

At their headquarters in Tokyo the Rissho-Kosei-kai hold a daily morning service which regularly attracts some 10 000 men and women. This is followed by a *hoza*, a group counselling session, at which the leader teaches and answers questions. Usually discussion focusses on practical issues such as health, bringing up children, improving one's personal relationships or how to find happiness. The headquarters also receives around 25 000 daily visitors, with the result that Rissho-Kosei-kai members have had to organise their own 'traffic police' at the entrance, equipped with armbands, flags and whistles to ensure that visitors are able to move around the premises in an orderly fashion.

The Reiyukai and the Rissho-Kosei-kai have few differences in their teachings, but differ in their emphases. The Rissho-Kosei-kai places more emphasis on the *sokaimyo* (inscription bearing ancestors' names) than on Gautama the Buddha. They perhaps incorporate more Shinto ancestor veneration than the Reiyukai, seeking to provide spiritual benefits for ancestors, rather than (as the Reiyukai do) allow ancestor remembrance to benefit those who live in the present.

From 1959 onwards the Rissho-Kosei-kai became actively involved politically and it began to emphasise the necessity of social welfare and overseas aid, achieving much by way of famine relief in Africa in particular. There are currently some two million members in Japan, and the high esteem with which this religious movement is held is reflected in the fact that their president was invited to attend the Second Vatican Council in 1965 as a non-Christian observer.

Nipponzan Myohoji

One further group which is worthy of comment is the Nipponzan Myohoji (sometimes called Nichihonzon Myohoji), founded by Nichidatsu Fujii (who died in 1985). A follower of Nichiren, Nichidatsu Fujii received ordination in 1903, at the age of 19, and began to preach publicly after the First World War. In 1924 he established his own school of Nichiren — called Nipponzon Myohoji — and he travelled widely, becoming a close acquaintance of Mahatma Gandhi when in India. During the Second World War he prayed and fasted for peace.

The holocaust of Hiroshima and Nagasaki intensified Nichidatsu Fujii's desire for peace, and he made a worldwide pilgrimage, establishing some 80 peace pagodas (or *stupas*). The aim was to create lasting peace through Buddhism, and thus the fundamental Buddhist principle of respect for life was sent out from the land of the first victims of nuclear warfare.

Some pagodas have been constructed for purely ornamental purposes, such as the famous one in Kew Gardens, London (which was not in fact constructed by Buddhists at all). However, when *stupas* were constructed for religious reasons they were originally containers of sacred relics, usually the remains of the dead. More recently, many have come to symbolise peace, harmony and compassion. Devotees will walk around the pagoda, symbolising the journey of spiritual advancement which they are attempting to make.

Some of the Nipponzan Myohoji pagodas are particularly worthy of mention. The year 1969 saw the completion of a peace pagoda at Rajgir, on the top of Mount Ratnagiri, the very spot where Taho in his treasure tower is believed to have descended upon Gautama and his large assembly of hearers. Mount Ratnagiri stands high, overlooking Vulture's Peak, a favourite platform used by the Buddha to proclaim the Dharma. Until recently, the site was almost inaccessible, but the Nipponzan Myohoji Order ensured that a road was built, and it is now possible to reach the site by means of a *tonga* — a horse and trap — which is the usual means of transport in this part of India. Visitors who do not wish to undertake a two-kilometre climb in the intense heat can avail themselves of a cable-car to make an effortless ascent.

Nichidatsu Fujii was responsible for the construction of two pagodas in Great Britain, one at Milton Keynes (completed in 1980) and another in Battersea Park, London. From 1951 the area of park-land had been used as a pleasure garden and fun-fair. The latter closed in 1974, following a serious roller-coaster accident, and a new purpose for the grounds had to be decided. Since the Greater London Council had designated 1983 as 'Peace Year', the Council welcomed the suggestion that the pagoda be constructed.

The Battersea pagoda is the most elaborate one ever erected by the Nipponzan Myohoji. The construction is of reinforced concrete, but Japanese craftsmen used their skills at sculpture, employing many oriental tools which were unfamiliar to British builders. Sacred relics of the Buddha were sent from Buddhists in Kathmandu, Burma, Sri Lanka and Japan, and were reverently placed inside the foundations.

At the official opening ceremony on 14 May 1985, Buddhists from all traditions were present, as well as representatives from most of the world's major traditions. Cardinal Hume spoke, representing the Roman Catholic Church, and Bishop Trevor Huddlestone read a message from the Archbishop of Canterbury.

Nipponzan Myohoji Peace Pagoda, Battersea Park, London
Photograph: George Chryssides.

Nichidatsu Fujii had expected that the London pagoda would be the last major work in his life for the cause of Buddhism and world peace. He did not live to see the inaugural ceremony, having died in Atami, Japan, on 9 January of that year. He was by then 100 years old.

Notes to Chapter 9

1   Jim Cowan (editor), *The Buddhism of the Sun* (NSUK, Richmond, Surrey, 1982) p 54
2   Senchu Murano, *The Sutra of the Lotus Flower of the Wonderful Law* (translation) (Nichiren Shu, Tokyo, Japan, 1974) ch 15
3   Jim Cowan, *op cit*, p 60
4   *Ibid*, p 58
5   *Ibid*, p 52. This passage summarises the first chapter of the *Vimalakirti Sutra*, a well known Mahayana scripture.
6   Diasaku Ikeda, 'The true eternity of life· A lecture' in Cowan, *op cit*, p 116

10

The Iron Bird Flies:
Buddhism and the West

When the iron bird flies,
    and horses run on wheels,
The Tibetan people will be scattered
    like ants across the World,
And the Dharma will come
    to the land of the Red Man.

So runs an ancient Tibetan prophecy. Like most prophecies
its precise meaning is unclear. Some Buddhists hold that it
refers to the Tibetan people, who used to paint their faces
red when preparing for war, and that the saying foretold
Buddhism's arrival in Tibet many centuries ago. A more
popular interpretation amongst Buddhists today, however,
is that it refers to the spreading of Buddhism westwards.
Some Buddhists believe that the 'Red Man' is the American
Indian and that the prophecy predicts the advent of Buddhism
in the USA. The iron bird sometimes has been thought to
mean the aeroplane, and the horse running on wheels is the
motor car, both of which were invented around the turn of
the century, almost coinciding with the British invasion
of Tibet in 1904. Of course the Tibetan people were not
scattered until half a century later, with the advance of the
Communist forces in 1959; nevertheless all these events are
roughly contemporary with the advent of Buddhism in the
West. Whatever the prophecy really means, Buddhism in all
its varieties has spread westwards and interacted with many
new cultures, ideologies and religions, not least of which is
Christianity.

Christian Missionaries Arrive

Apart from inaccurate hearsay, Christianity's first knowledge of Buddhism was gleaned from the Christian missionaries and from the translations and writings of scholars. The nineteenth century saw the beginnings of the vast undertaking of making Buddhist scriptures available to the West, principally in English, German and French. Of the translators, the most influential was Eugene Burnouf (1854–1920), who translated and edited the Lotus Sutra in 1852. Also important was Hermann Oldenberg (1854–1920), a German, who edited the complete *Pali Vinaya-pitaka*; while in England, T W Rhys Davids (1843–1922) was extremely productive in his translation work and founded the Pali Text Society in 1881. At this stage, western interest in Buddhism was largely academic and few westerners actually embraced Buddhism.

Another source of introduction to Buddhist ideas was through English 'transcendentalist' poets such as Emerson and Blake, who used ideas derived from Buddhism. Edwin Arnold's epic poem, *The Light of Asia* (1879), recounted in English verse the story of the birth, enlightenment and mission of the Buddha. This was a literary landmark for Buddhism: the one-way system of traffic between westerners and Buddhists was soon to change.

During the nineteenth century the attitude of the Christian missionaries towards Buddhism was one of disapproval, and often outright hostility. Hindus, among others, had permitted Buddhists to practise their religion in conjunction with their own faith, believing that there was no conflict, but for the Christians the idea of following more than one religion at a time was (and still is) totally unacceptable. Protestant missionaries were especially offended by the use of images of buddhas and bodhisattvas as aids to devotion. These were often viewed as 'idols' or 'graven images', and were seen as a serious breach of the second of the Ten Commandments. As Reginald Heber wrote in his famous hymn 'From Greenland's icy mountains':

In vain with lavish kindness
    The gifts of God are strewn;
The heathen in his blindness
    Bows down to wood and stone.

The missionaries seem to have found it hard to accept that Hindus and Buddhists do not worship the images themselves but what they represent. The Revd George Smith, later Bishop of Hong Kong, has this to say about his missionary encounters with the Buddhist faith:

> I was disturbed at an early hour by a [Buddhist] priest groaning in the ante-room and uttering doleful sounds, as he prostrated his body before the hideous idol, after relighting the perfume sticks. I remonstrated with the poor creature, who, with a vacant stare, asked me whether there were no Buddhist priests in my own country, and what idols we worshipped. I gave him a tract, which he was unable to read, and which I therefore received again. In the afternoon I passed through some lesser temples, in which a few priests were performing their customary mummeries.[1]

Smith implies that many of the Sangha were illiterate, but we are not told in what language the tract was written (it would almost certainly have been English), and this may explain the monk's difficulty. Smith goes on to describe how he continued to hand out to Buddhist monks, while they were meditating, tracts which 'contained a remonstrance against the sin of idolatry'. Later, in a small temple, he attempted to show the senselessness of 'idol worship' by poking the 'ugly idols' with his umbrella. He records:

> As I gave them a slight thrust they trembled, tottered, and tumbled from their thrones. The people again laughed heartily, as the priests tried for some time in vain to make one of the idols maintain its sitting posture, the fall having disordered its component parts. Thinking that this liberty might put their good humour to too severe a test, I became more serious in my manner, and spoke of the wrath of God on those who thus dishonour his name.[2]

The Great Debate of Panadura

At the time of the missionary hey-day, Christian–Buddhist relationships were very strained, to say the least. In Sri Lanka (formerly Ceylon), Buddhists believed that the Christian presence discriminated against them. Children had to be educated in Christian schools and only Christian holidays were recognised by the government. If children absented themselves to celebrate Buddhist festivals, they were punished. In the law courts, Buddhists were obliged to swear on the Christian Bible that they would not perjure themselves. Although Buddhist processions were tolerated, the use of the drum and other musical accompaniments was banned.

Missionaries often failed to recognise that Buddhism confronted them with a much older religious tradition than theirs—a religion which had its own scriptures and which was very deeply embedded in the cultures in which it had taken root. Relatively few converts to Christianity were gained; Christianity had much greater success in countries like Africa with its non-literate tribal religions which contrasted markedly with the scholarly tradition of the Buddhist faith.

By viewing Buddhism as primitive and superstitious, Christian missionaries underestimated the ability of the Buddhist Sangha to argue its case forcibly against them. One Protestant missionary, the Revd David de Silva made anti-Buddhist comments in a sermon preached in Sri Lanka in 1873. The Buddhists took exception to his remarks and requested him to state publicly his objections to Buddhism and to dispute with them. A time and place was set and so the Great Debate of Panadura occurred in August 1873.

It was an impressive occasion. Protestants of all denominations—Baptists, Wesleyans and clergy from the Church Missionary Society—turned out in force. The Revd David de Silva and a new Christian convert, Mr F S Sirinamme, prepared to speak on behalf of the Christians. The Ven Migettuwatte Gunananda, a formidable scholar, was the spokesman for the Buddhists, and he brought with him some 200 members of the Sangha. An enormous crowd of five or six thousand had assembled in the early hours of the morning, determined not to miss this momentous event. Sinhalese youths made their way around the congregation selling refreshments (sherbet and roasted chick-peas), and the police were present to keep order.

The Great Debate lasted for two days, with morning and afternoon sessions of two hours apiece. De Silva began the debate, attacking, amongst other issues, the Buddhist notion that there are no souls, enquiring how rebirth was possible if this was so. However, de Silva spent much of his time simply explaining to the audience the basic teachings of Buddhism. In order to convince his audience that his facts were right, he quoted lengthy passages from Buddhist scriptures in the original Pali (long since a dead language) and it is doubtful whether more than a mere handful of the audience understood him.

Ven Gunananda, by contrast, was better able to address a crowd of ordinary people. Not only was he a competent Buddhist scholar, but he had read the Bible thoroughly too, even quoting some very obscure passages with which, in all probability, most Christians today are unfamiliar. He posed many penetrating questions to de Silva: why is God described as 'jealous'?; how could an all-powerful God ever have to 'repent' of making humankind?; why did Jephthah kill his own daughter as a sacrifice to God?; why did the Bible suggest in some places that salvation was gained by faith, and in other places by deeds? For Gunananda it was illogical to believe that Jesus rose from the dead: his disciples must have stolen his body. De Silva had cast aspersions on the morality of certain members of the Sangha, noting that some of the leading figures in Buddhist history had been murderers. 'What about Moses?' Gunananda objected in return, 'The Bible not only records that he killed the Egyptian, but condones it. At least in the Buddhist tradition the murderers who became enlightened repented of their misdeeds.'

By inviting de Silva to begin the debate, Gunananda had thereby ensured that he had the last word. As he dealt his final blows to Christianity, he was greeted with cries of '*Sadhu!*' from the crowd, meaning 'Excellent!' The missionaries had failed to convince their audience and the Buddhists were judged to have won the day.

Colonel Olcott and the Buddhist Revival in Ceylon (Sri Lanka)

A full account of the debate, containing the text of the speeches, translated into English, appeared in the *Ceylon Times*. This issue of the journal was seen by an American, Colonel Henry Steel Olcott, and Olcott's discovery was a landmark in Sinhalese Buddhist history.

Olcott (1832–1907) was a soldier who fought in the American Civil War, aspiring to the rank of Colonel. Having completed his military service, he became a successful lawyer in New York. His contacts with Buddhism began when he was commissioned to investigate a case involving a new religious group. He was actually impressed by what he saw there, and decided that he wanted to study more. In the group he met Madame Blavatsky and they jointly became the founders of the Theosophical Society. (Theosophy seeks to discover unexplained laws and powers in the world, and encourages the study of religions, especially Buddhism, in order to find an ancient secret wisdom which lies at their core.) Olcott and Blavatsky set out for India in 1878, eventually reaching Sri Lanka in 1880. When Olcott read the account of the Great Debate of Panadura, he concluded that the Buddhists had gained the victory. In 1880, he and Madame Blavatsky took the Three Refuges and Five Precepts.

Olcott wanted to ensure that Buddhists could practise their faith unimpeded, and founded a Theosophical Society in Sri Lanka, with the aim of preserving Buddhism. He established a number of Buddhist schools providing free education for children. Because of the zeal of the Christian missionaries, Buddhists had become somewhat demoralised, and children, laity and even monks did not know their tradition as well as previous generations had done. Olcott compiled a *Buddhist Catechism* in 1881 to enable better understanding of Buddhism: it proved somewhat difficult for children and a simpler one had to be devised for them.

On Easter Day in 1883, a procession of Buddhists was organised. Opponents of Buddhism used physical violence to prevent it and at least one Buddhist participant was killed. This event caused Buddhists to set up a Buddhist Defence Committee, which prevailed upon Olcott to visit London and plead the cause of Buddhism to the Secretary of State for the Colonies. Olcott's visit bore various results which pleased the Sinhalese Buddhists. From then on, Buddhists were allowed to act as registrars for marriages, Buddhist witnesses in the courts were no longer obliged to take the Christian oath, and Buddhist festivals were recognised as public holidays. As a symbol of the resurgence of Buddhism against western colonialism, Olcott designed a Buddhist flag, which proved acceptable to Buddhists of all traditions, and is still used today.

Olcott also visited Japan, lecturing widely on Buddhism and aiding a Buddhist revival there also. He devised a set of 'Fourteen Fundamental Buddhistic Beliefs' which was endorsed by all major schools with which he made contact — namely Theravada, Pure Land, Zen and Nichiren. (Olcott did not meet Tibetan Buddhists.) Interestingly, the sixth point of his Buddhist creed contains a thinly disguised criticism of the Christian missionaries' message:

> Ignorance also begets the illusive and illogical idea that there is only one existence for man, and the other illusion that this one life is followed by [a] state of unchangeable pleasure or torment.[3]

Olcott died in 1907, near Madras in India. His corpse was taken to the cremation ground, swathed in the Buddhist flag which he had designed, together with the 'stars and stripes' flag of his home country.

Anagarika Dharmapala (David Hewavitarne, 1864–1933)

Anagarika Dharmapala was a Sinhalese Buddhist who was highly influential in the development of modern Buddhism. His given name was David Hewavitarne and he was born into a Buddhist family in Colombo. He disliked the missionary presence, which he described as 'Christian barbarism'. He met Colonel Olcott in 1891, became his student and subsequently sought ordination as a Buddhist monk. In the same year, he visited Bodh Gaya, the site of the Buddha's enlightenment, and was dismayed by the state of neglect in which he found the place. In order to work for its restoration, he founded the Mahabodhi Society in Colombo. Although Buddhism has a strong tradition of meditation, the practice had almost died out. Dharmapala discovered a manuscript of an old handbook on Buddhist meditation when he visited a monastery at Bambaragala. This was later published by the Pali Text Society and translated as the *Manual of a Mystic*. Teachings on meditation were thus re-discovered. In Burma, too, a monk called Narada restored the practice of 'awareness of mindfulness', and so a new Burmese tradition of meditation was established.

Buddhism in the USA

While some westerners made contact with Buddhism as a result of journeys to the East, easterners also migrated westward, bringing their religions with them. Buddhism first came to the West with Chinese immigrants to California, who were attracted by the Gold Rush in the 1840s. They were mainly Pure Land Buddhists, and came as members of the laity without bringing priests with them. When they settled, they established 'joss-houses' (as their Chinese temples were called), where they met to perform their devotions. (The name 'joss-house' was given, of course, because of the burning of incense, or 'joss-sticks'.) Devotions were not exclusively Buddhist but often a mixture of Chinese ancestor veneration, cults of popular Chinese deities, and Chinese forms of Buddhism. Many temples were dedicated to the bodhisattva Kuan Yin. (Kuan Yin is the female form of Avalokiteshvara in Chinese Buddhism; she is called 'Kwannon' in Japan.)

When the Japanese came to San Francisco, arriving via Hawaii, they not only brought Pure Land Buddhism but Pure Land priests as well. This provided Buddhists and other seekers with a more organised form of Buddhism, with more precise and definitive explanations of it. California is well known as the seed-bed of new religious ideas and Buddhism gained a number of western followers.

The Parliament of Religions

As Buddhism came into contact with other faiths in the United States, particularly Christianity, one very notable event took place in 1893. This was the World Parliament of Religions in Chicago. A staggering assembly of some 7000 representatives of all the major religious traditions of the world met 'to bring together in conference for the first time in history the leading representatives of the historic religions of the world'. The purpose was not inter-religious confrontation, as had occurred in Sri Lanka, but mutual understanding and learning. Although Buddhism was represented, it was mainly a selection of the Mahayana schools which attended, with a few Theravadins; no Tibetan Buddhists were present at all—the distance was no doubt too great and they may not have been aware that the Parliament was meeting.

A further goal of the World Parliament was 'to show…in the most impressive way, what and how many important truths the various religions hold and teach in common'. Despite this well-intentioned aim, much of the discussion at the Parliament focussed on religious differences as well as similarities. There was certainly no attempt to pretend that all religions basically were expressing the same truths, or that any should compromise in order to create some new global religion containing elements of all the faiths which were present. The common interest was, rather, on sharing what each religion believed it had to offer, and to discover what light each shed on the problems facing humankind, particularly the quest for permanent international peace.

Two notable Buddhists, among others, spoke at the Parliament. One was Anagarika Dharmapala, Olcott's student and fellow worker from Sri Lanka, and another was Soen Shaku, a Zen Master of the Rinzai tradition. Paul Carus (1852–1919), an influential publisher, was inspired by Soen Shaku, and invited Daisetz Teitaro Suzuki (1870–1966), Soen Shaku's pupil, to work for his publishing company. Suzuki was a prolific writer and did more than any other Zen teacher to make Zen accessible to a western popular readership. From about 1920 onwards, his works were read widely, and they are still readily available in bookshops.

Buddhism in Britain

In 1905, R J Jackson became the first practising English Buddhist, and began to lecture on Buddhism from a soapbox in Regent's Park. Together with J R Pain, an ex-soldier from Burma, they established a bookshop for the sale of Buddhist literature, and developed their Regent's Park lecture programme, having painted their portable platform orange, with the motto, 'The Word of the Glorious Buddha is sure and everlasting'. Sizeable crowds attended the lectures.

In the meantime, an Englishman called Allan Bennett had travelled to Burma and become ordained as a Buddhist monk under the name of Ananda Metteyya. From Burma he spearheaded a Buddhist mission to England, arriving back on St George's Day in 1908. The tide was turning. It was not long before a Buddhist Society was founded with its headquarters in London, representing all schools of Buddhism.

The year 1925 saw the arrival in England of Anagarika Dharmapala from Sri Lanka. Dharmapala's mission presented traditional Theravada Buddhism to England, which is probably its best known form.

One of Jackson's converts, Francis Payne, delivered a series of lectures on Buddhism in 1923 in the Essex Hall, the Strand. These lectures were attended by Christmas Humphreys, a lawyer, who became one of the leading and most prolific exponents of Buddhism in the West. Like Colonel Olcott, Humphreys was a Theosophist, and he formed a Buddhist Lodge within The Theosophical Society in 1924. This eventually developed into the Buddhist Society, which exists today in Central London. Humphreys travelled widely, particularly during the Second World War, when he was asked to take part in the prosecution of Japanese war criminals. (Humphreys also made himself controversial in Buddhist circles, being the prosecuting counsel in the trial of Ruth Ellis, the last person to be hanged in the UK.) In his travels, Humphreys did much to assist Buddhists in other countries, and, in the style of Olcott, he devised 'Twelve Principles of Buddhism' which he circulated to Buddhists of different traditions as he met them. Humphreys' Twelve Principles of Buddhism proved acceptable to most communities, although not all. Humphreys' own favoured brand of Buddhism was Zen but The Buddhist Society represents all schools.

In the 1950s the Sangha founded a residence within Britain, with Sinhalese Buddhists opening the London Vihara in 1954. The year 1962 saw the establishment in Hampstead, London, of the first *vihara* in the United Kingdom which accepted British candidates for ordination. This was a very traditional Theravadin order, coming from a Thai community who lived in forest huts. It has now moved to the forests of Hampshire. Since then, many varieties of Buddhism have gained momentum in Britain, and today there are around 180 groups of practising Buddhists, although some of these are very small.

Tibetan Buddhism in the West

As a result of the Chinese occupation of Tibet in 1959, refugee lamas came to the United States and to Europe. Of the Tibetan refugee teachers, two are particularly note-worthy. Tarthang Tulku was chosen by the Dalai Lama as a teacher of the Nyingmapa ('ancient') tradition at the Institute of Higher Tibetan Studies at the Sanskrit University of Varanasi. He gave up the robe before emigrating to the USA in 1968, where he established the Nyingmapa Meditation Centre in Berkeley and the Tibetan Relief Foundation, among various other religious projects.

Chogyam Trungpa (1939–87) came to Britain and founded the Samye-ling Monastery in Dumfriesshire. This was the first Tibetan monastery ever established outside Tibet. After a serious car accident in 1969, Trungpa gave up the robe and emigrated to the States where he founded the Karme Choling ('Tail of the Tiger') Meditation Centre, and the Naropa Institute in Boulder, Colorado. He was a prolific writer, and did much to transpose traditional Tibetan ideas into a western setting. The Samye-ling Monastery continues to exist, and an impressive temple is under construction, due to open in 1988.

In the Gelugpa tradition is the Lam Rim Buddhist Centre in Wales, set in eight acres of ground, with a resident Tibetan teacher. The Manjushri Institute near Conishead in the Lake District was converted from a Christian priory: it now has two resident Tibetan lamas and is used for the training of *geshes*. (A *geshe* is someone who has undergone extensive training in Tibetan religion and philosophy. The programme of study takes nine years—longer in Tibet itself—and is sometimes said to be equivalent to a western doctorate.)

The Westernisation of Buddhism

When a religion arrives in a new or foreign culture, changes are inevitable. Religions adapt to new environments, and Buddhism has proved in the past to be eminently capable of changing its outward form to accommodate the cultures it has met. Are we therefore likely to see new forms of Buddhism in the West as Buddhism absorbs western ideas?

One Buddhist movement which is dedicated to finding

The Samye Ling Monastery, Dumfriesshire (under construction)
© *Kagyu Samye Ling, Tibetan Centre, Eskdalemuir, Dumfriesshire, Scotland. Reproduced by permission.*

such a new form is the Western Buddhist Order (WBO). The Order was founded in 1968 by Ven Sangharakshita, a former English army conscript who served in India during the War, and tore up his papers to take on the robe and follow the Buddhist path. The Western Buddhist Order is highly critical of those western Buddhists who, it claims, have treated Buddhism as a kind of 'hobby'. These Buddhists have taken up the study of the religion and some of the meditative practices, but have lived a typically western lifestyle, drinking alcohol, eating meat and wearing furs. As Sangharakshita has said, 'a difference must make a difference' and, for example, 'Buddhism and beefsteaks do not go together'.

This much is traditional. What is less traditional is the financing of the movement, which does not look for alms, but has moved 'from beggars to business' by setting up a number of commercial enterprises, stressing the fifth point of the Eightfold Path — 'perfect livelihood'. The movement is also open in principle to Buddhist teachings finding a new form of expression which is amenable to the West. It has already expressed a commitment to *individual* growth, in contrast to the traditional doctrine that there are 'no selves'. For such reasons, not all Buddhists applaud the WBO's attempts at adaptation.

Adaptations in the West

The WBO is not the first example of the westernisation of Buddhism. We have already seen westernisation occurring as Buddhists responded to the Christian missionaries. As Buddhism revived to fight back, it set itself up as 'the religion of reason'. One consequence of this was that Buddhists tended to jettison superstitions and accounts of miracles within their own tradition.

Another way of adapting to the West was to create organisations similar to those of Christianity. There were Sunday Schools for Buddhist children (later renamed 'Dharma Schools'), Buddhist catechisms and creeds, and organisations such as the Young Men's Buddhist Association in the USA, India, Sri Lanka and elsewhere. Some Buddhist teachers in the USA began to be called 'priests', and the leader of one large Buddhist organisation was actually referred to as a Buddhist 'bishop'. Christianity had made its mark, although perhaps not quite in the way the Christian missionaries had expected.

We have seen how the Christian presence caused Buddhists to recover their tradition of meditation. However, westernisation caused several important changes. In the East it is normal for Buddhists to meditate or engage in devotion in the company of members of their own tradition, even though there is inter-mingling of ideas. In the West this is not always possible, particularly in rural areas where only a few Buddhists reside, spanning a variety of traditions. Consequently, western Buddhists often come together and meditate en masse, each in his or her own preferred way. This contrasts with the eastern tradition where there is normally a one-to-one relationship between the meditation teacher and the pupil, and where the teacher acts almost as a kind of psychologist, offering advice to the pupil based on what he or she observes. An eastern teacher will observe the pupil carefully, taking note of how even menial tasks are performed — such as sweeping a floor — and will instruct accordingly. Not only is this barely possible in the West, owing to the scarcity of accredited teachers, but westerners appear to prefer group meditation to the traditional eastern master-pupil relationship.

It is difficult to see whether any substantially new form of Buddhism is in sight. Some Buddhists have spoken of a 'Navayana'—a new vehicle—which will emerge in the West. Others have attempted to create an 'Ekayana'—a single vehicle—which combines ideas from all Buddhist schools in an ecumenical way. As yet, however, no Navayana or Ekayana has established itself as a firm presence within Buddhism. Only time will tell whether some new form of Buddhism will arise. If Buddhism changes as a result of its encounters with the West, this would be consistent with its fundamental doctrine of *anicca* (impermanence). Everything changes—and this applies to the forms of Buddhism themselves. As Christmas Humphreys wrote:

Why should there not be in time a Western Buddhism...? There is no reason why it should not grow happily alongside, and even blend with the best of Western science, psychology and social science, and thus affect the everchanging field of Western thought. It will not be Theravada or Zen, Prajnaparamita intuitive philosophy or Tibetan ritual. Just what it will be we do not know, nor does it matter at the present time. The Dharma as such is immortal, but its forms must ever change to serve the everchanging human need.[4]

Notes to Chapter 10

1   Quoted in Holmes Welch, *The Buddhist Revival in China* (Harvard University Press, Cambridge, Massachussetts, USA, 1968) pp 224–225
2   Holmes Welch, *ibid*
3   B P Kirthioinghc and M P Amarasurıya, *Colonel Olcott: His Service to Buddhism* (Buddhist Publication Society, Kandy, Sri Lanka, 1981) p 15
4   Christmas Humphreys, *Sixty Years of Buddhism in England* (The Buddhist Society, London, 1968) p 80

Further Reading

Heinz Bechert and Richard Gombrich (editors), *The World of Buddhism* (Thames and Hudson Ltd, London, 1984). Although very expensive, Bechert and Gombrich's book is comprehensive and lavishly illustrated.

Christmas Humphreys, *Buddhism* (Penguin Books Ltd, Middlesex, 1951). Humphrey's introduction was the first to popularise Buddhism in the UK. It is still a bestseller.

Juan Mascaro, *The Dhammapada* (translation) (Penguin Books Ltd, Middlesex, 1973). Although there are many editions of *The Dhammapada*, this version is the most readily available.

Peggy Morgan, *Buddhism in the Twentieth Century* (Amersham, Hulton, 1985). This is a very short introductory overview of Buddhism, focussing on the theme of messengers, scriptures, worship, pilgrimage and festivals.

Walpole Rahula, *What the Buddha Taught* (Gordon Fraser, London, 1978). An introduction to Buddhist doctrine from the Thervada tradition.

A Solé-Leris, *Tranquility and Insight* (Rider & Co, London, 1986). This book is about Buddhist meditation.

Glossary

Amitabha: The Buddha of Infinite Light, worshipped particularly by Pure Land Buddhists.

Anatta: 'No self' — the doctrine that there is no soul. One of the three Marks of Existence.

Anicca: Impermanence — One of the three Marks of Existence.

Arhut. One who is enlightened.

Avalokiteshvara: The *bodhisattva* of compassion.

Bhikkhu: A Theravadin monk.

Bodhisattva: One who has gained enlightenment, but who renounces final entry into *nirvana* in order to help other living beings.

Brahmin: The top Hindu caste (teacher-priests).

Buddha: One who has gained enlightenment.

Chenrezig: Tibetan name of Avalokiteshvara.

Dalai Lama: The spiritual leader of the Tibetan Buddhists and head of the Gelugpa school.

Dhammapada: One of the best known early Buddhist scriptures.

Dharma: The teaching of the Buddha.

Dukkha: Unsatisfactoriness — one of the three Marks of Existence.

Gohonzon: The scroll which is the principal object of devotion in the Nichiren sects.

Gongyo: A Nichiren ceremony, consisting of chanting before the *gohonzon* (see above).

Hinayana: Literally 'Lesser Vehicle' — an abusive term applied to those Buddhists who are not Mahayana.

Jatakas: Stories of the previous lives of the Buddha.

Jodo: A form of Pure Land Buddhism, which flourished in China and Japan.

Karma: Deeds. The law of *karma* asserts that everyone will eventually experience the effects of his or her actions.

Koan: In Zen, a problem which the student is given and to which there is no logical answer.

Lotus Sutra: A Mahayana scripture, to which Nichiren Buddhists attach particular significance.

Mahayana: Literally 'Greater Vehicle' — the forms of Buddhism which dominated in Tibet, China, Korea and Japan.

Manjushri: The *bodhisattva* of wisdom, often regarded as the chief of the *bodhisattvas*.

Mantra: Sacred words which are chanted and believed to have great power.

Marks of Existence: Features of everything in the universe, often called 'Signs of Being' — *anicca, anatta, dukkha*.

'Nam myoho renge kyo':   'Homage to the Lotus Sutra'; the *mantra* which, according to Nichiren Buddhists, encapsulates the whole of that scripture.

Nembutsu: Recitation of Amitabha's name. Japanese name for Pure Land Buddhism.

Nichiren Daishonin: The founder of the Nichiren school of Buddhism in thirteenth century Japan.

Nirvana: Enlightenment — the supreme goal of the Buddhist, after attaining which one is no longer reborn.

Parinirvana: The Buddha's death after attaining *nirvana*, after which there would be no rebirth.

Prajna: Wisdom.

Roshi: A Zen Master (of either sex).

Samsara: The cycle of birth and rebirth.

Sangha: The community of monks. One of the Three Jewels.

Satori: Enlightenment (used only in Zen).

Sesshin: A period of retreat for intensive meditation (Zen tradition).

Shakubuku: Literally 'break and subdue' — the winning of converts in the Nichiren Shoshu sect.

Shakyamuni: The clan name of Siddhartha Gautama, the Buddha.

Siddha: A religious figure (usually a recluse) who has gained magical powers (Tibetan tradition).

Siddhartha Gautama: The personal name of the historical Buddha.

Stupa: A monument which usually contains relics and which is an object of devotion.

Sukhavati: The Pure Land or celestial paradise of the Buddhas.

Sutra: A scripture recording a sermon preached by the Buddha.

Taho: The second Buddha, mentioned in the Lotus Sutra, who descended in his 'treasure tower' to join Gautama.

Tendai: A form of Buddhism similar to and pre-dating Zen.

Theravada: Literally 'teaching of the Elders' — the form of Hinayana Buddhism which survives in Sri Lanka and South East Asia.

Three Jewels, or Triple Gem: The Buddha, Dharma and Sangha.

Three Refuges: Buddha, Dharma and Sangha.

Vajrayana: The 'Diamond Vehicle'; the form of Buddhism which flourished in Tibet.

Vihara: Literally, 'dwelling place' — a building which houses the Sangha.

Vipassana: 'Insight' meditation.

Wesak: The festival marking the Buddha's enlightenment.

Yidam: An image which one is given to 'visualise', particularly in the Vajrayana tradition.

Yoga: Spiritual path.

Yogi: A meditator.

Zazen: Meditation in the Zen tradition.